The
SCHOOL ZONE
MENTALITY

The SCHOOL ZONE MENTALITY

Raise Thriving Kids by
Slowing Down in Five Everyday Zones

Natalie Gonzalez

2025

The School Zone Mentality: Raise Thriving Kids by Slowing Down in Five Everyday Zones
Copyright 2025 Natalie Gonzalez

For information: http://www.theschoolzonementality.com/

The author does not represent the information herein as legal, medical, or other professional advice. This book is not a substitute for professional advice.

Author photo on page 151 by Randy Peterson, https://www.thedistillerymedia.com/

ISBN: 979-8-9988731-0-2

CONTENTS

TO ASHER JAMES AND OLIVIA JOY...

YOU ARE MY SUNSHINE.

IN LOVING MEMORY OF BIGGIE.

INTRODUCTION

I hadn't even delivered my first child before the tugs of cultural norms around parenting inundated my decisions and musings about motherhood. Without the felt experience of raising a child—an extension of yourself, yet another soul—it was easy enough to yield to the typical notions around the dos and don'ts of parenting.

I had very little experience with children (ironic, I realize, as the author of a book about raising children), so going with the flow seemed OK for the most part. But the longer I do this, the more kids and parents I meet, and the more I observe the world around us via community events, social media, and the news, the harder it hits: The kids are not all right.

We can scapegoat a handful of monumental events in the last decade that make it tough for a lot of us to feel like we have our feet underneath us. But the sociologist in me realizes that something foundational is off. Sure, acts of domestic terrorism and global pandemics are bound to impact this generation in ways we haven't yet measured (though some data is immediately revealing pervasive trauma that should absolutely warrant its own conversation... elsewhere, though). On a microlevel, however, in interactions between children and parents, as well as among their peers, there are clear, alarming signs that something is amiss. Something we're doing isn't working... or worse, some things we're doing are causing catastrophic results.

SLOWING DOWN

One weekday morning as I was driving my kids to school through a school zone, it occurred to me that this is the perfect metaphor for what it's going to take to cultivate different, better outcomes for our kids. (Thus, you understand now what the heck school zones have to do with all this.) We need more metaphorical school zones, and we need them in very strategic areas.

School zones function to protect our children for several key reasons:

- We've decided that kids are worth protecting in this capacity
- We slow down
- This intervention actually works
- We all do it, everyone in the community

The major thoroughfares on the roadmap for raising children are therefore what I'll refer to as "zones," thinking about expanding our concept of school zones to other pathways throughout the lives of young people that will ensure they stay safe and well. By paving and understanding—via science and life lessons alike—these various zones, we can forge a different kind of childhood and a different kind of culture. One in which kids are honored as distinctively not-adults, in which parents are equipped with knowledge that describes what children truly need, and in which we take responsibility for reversing a status quo that harms kids and maims families.

BRINGING ZONES INTO OUR HOMES

Most of you picking up this book already spot the signals warning of danger ahead, either in your own household or in one you care about. As with any challenge, acknowledging the problem is the first step. But then what? Are kids today too far gone? Are parents too irrelevant? Is this the new normal?

In short: Heck, no.

What we're missing today in most of our homes and communities is a modern, research-driven framework for raising thriving children on all fronts: physically, mentally, spiritually, and emotionally. Several decades ago, we didn't have access to the kind of research into child development, neuroscience, and behavioral studies that we do today. (This is the part where we take a deep breath and give our collective selves—and those who came before us—some grace.)

But very few parents can find the time to pore over the many books, journals, articles, and podcasts that reveal these findings for the very audience who can best harness their insights and power. Cruel plot twist, right?

As I've mentioned, I'm earning my spurs "on the job," knee deep in the elementary years with now two precious kiddos. When those babes were placed in my arms, some of the conventional guidelines around how you raise and care for babies started to feel... off.

I struggled with the shame I felt that breastfeeding was such a beatdown, that my son was so small that we had to stay an extra day in the hospital after delivery (see: breastfeeding beatdown), that I couldn't get him to sleep through the night right off the bat, that "drowsy but awake" seemed like a mirage and I despaired with every begrudging contact nap.

Little by little, I found my own way, though. I ignored the baby books, I stopped Googling, and I observed my children. I responded to them, I learned from them, and I discovered a confidence that truly didn't make sense given I was still a total newbie at this whole mom thing.

What surprised me more than anything, and what I can't wait to share with you, is that the intuitive stuff aligned beautifully with what research instructs for raising children and cultivating a family. Each "rule" I discarded, inherited from Western advice on rearing kids, turned out to be inherently flawed and discarded for very good reasons.

And herein lies the discovery that I want to share with you: There is a roadmap for raising children well. The milestones are relatively simple, and they're hidden in plain sight.

The "School Zone Mentality" represents a reframing of how we look at the landscape of our families. It's a mindset shift that encourages us to reconsider where we focus and protect our kids on a large scale. This is the work of communities, not just individuals.

Think about your neighborhood school zone; it doesn't work if everyone doesn't yield and comply. We must proceed slowly and intentionally. We understand why the zones exist, so we abide and uphold these sacred crossings.

We must now expand this mentality to establish and reinforce other zones at home, in schools, and throughout our communities (online and in person) that are paved via data-driven interventions and practices to provide safe passage for our most vulnerable. The decision to establish and uphold these zones isn't neutral. Like any good thing, it requires resolve and intention. But so does watching generations before us struggle with mental health, with worth, and with drive to be part of something bigger, to matter beyond their myopic youth.

THE FIVE ZONES

Together we'll focus on five zones that serve as the key milestones of this informed framework for raising kids well: diet and mealtimes, sleep practices, media consumption, schedules and rhythms, and physical spaces and possessions. Some of these chapters will be easier than others, and we'll all come with our own unique triggers and raw spots.

But in a not-so-surprising turn of events, we'll discover that what is beneficial for kids is also a win for the grown-ups. Be patient with yourself (and with the rest of your family), remembering that going against the status quo takes heart. I'll embolden you along the way with encouragement, anecdotes, and plenty of reliable references to keep your foot on the gas.

My prayer for this book is to serve as a call to action to hit the brakes on what isn't serving our children—or adults, in most cases—and to pave the way with approaches and strategies that are shown to enable children to thrive. We're going to heed the signals, forge new roads, and change the traffic pattern to deter the flow of traffic that is damaging our young people and threatening our shared future.

By establishing these zones (or perhaps reinforcing them), we can create runways for healthy childhoods that account for more than simply the walk to and from school. Kids need support every step of their day, for many years, to thrive and grow into who they are meant to be: holistically healthy adults who continue to honor children in return. And we have the privilege of sharing in this high calling, adult-to-adult, in whatever role we play in a child's life: parent, soon-to-be-parent, caregiver, relative, volunteer, policy-maker, step-whatever, and so on. This isn't only for biological parents. My invitation is for any caregiver, aunt/uncle, relative, friend, teacher, and babysitter to get in the zone with us, positively impacting your communities by starting on the microlevel: with a child that you love.

We're going to learn from child-development experts, neuroscientists, fellow sociologists, and wise parents who've been-there-done-that, motivating us forward and sharing practical steps for creating school zone-like areas throughout our homes and communities. And we're going to start with yours and mine.

Much of what we cover may seem like common sense, but we'll infuse the science into why Mama's known best all along. You'll also see that we as parents need to hold one another accountable for what is happening to our kids and support one another toward establishing new norms.

Again, this isn't just about protecting our own families, though we certainly start there. Seeing the fruit of these efforts should inspire you to share, to pay it forward, and to advocate for bigger macrochanges to shift the status quo. This is the "no kid left behind" movement that reverses troubling trends and gives our society legs on which to stand firmly and wholly.

Some of what I share may not jibe with the common advice we get from pediatricians or what we see implemented in public schools, and while this may cause some discomfort, you'll soon learn that research and the accompanying data is often available for years—decades, even—before it informs policies for large institutions like healthcare and school systems. We're getting ahead of the curve here, and I hope you'll stick with me on the road of a trailblazer, forging the path for what is to come and ensuring the children we love don't get run over by the status quo.

CHAPTER RESOURCES

In each chapter, I will include a few sections to encourage your path forward in the zones we cover. Because so much incredible work has been done in the parenting and wellness realm, I am not going to recreate the wheel nor take credit for said work. I will share resources to encourage additional study and context for areas of interest, and highly recommend those that I share, having leveraged them in my own ongoing journey raising my babies.

GET IN THE ZONE

These sections include highlights from the chapter, serving as a quick reference point for implementing that chapter's zone. Think of it as CliffsNotes for the topic at hand! These are mindset shifts or action steps that you can implement one at a time to establish sustainable changes in your household.

Each bullet provides value, but don't feel like you need to treat these sections as To Do lists, checking off every item before you can call it a win. Every step forward is worth celebrating. Don't forget to make these changes right alongside your children for them to really stick and benefit the whole family. What's good for the goose is often good for the gander.

CROSSING GUARDS

In keeping with our school zone metaphor, "Crossing Guards" are books, websites, social media accounts, or podcasts that provide deeper insight into the topics discussed. These are sources of reliable data and practical inspiration. You may not have the time to engage with all of them, but they're worth knowing about. You may see some Guards listed multiple times in various sections. If that resource doesn't pique your interest in one zone, it may for another. (They're also just that good.)

You don't have to go this journey alone, and I've found that the more tools I have in my toolbox from the rich content out there in many of these facets of child-rearing, the easier it is for me to engage when I am low on sleep and patience. We learn via repetition, so if a given chapter really resonates with you, capitalize on that interest and pick a Crossing Guard to continue your study and encourage you forward.

STICK THE LANDING

In gymnastics, there is a ton of focus on the landing. How did the gymnast finish? Did they "stick it"—solid footing, no wobbles—or did they falter? I know that we as caretakers want to nail this thing, but we would do well to remind ourselves that there is no actual training for this. No gym for building our parenting muscles, no benchmark by which we can measure our performance. Some days it feels pretty dang close to a 10.0, while other days we're limping through with a generous 3.5. We don't have to strive for perfection, but we are going for progress.

Your ability to stick the landing on implementing action steps, shifting family rhythms, and influencing the peers and caregivers around you will be determined by how much grace you allow yourself, how willing you are to acknowledge and react to new information (we'll cover this more in the next chapter), and how well you handle setbacks.

So let me start by reminding you that the goal isn't a perfect 10.0 from all the judges. Let's shoot for an 8.0 from our own inner judge, knowing they're often much harder on us than deserved, and let's celebrate every attempt at landing... even if we don't stick it the first time.

This is not the kind of book you need to finish all at once, nor is there a need to tackle all the zones at once. In fact, it's often easier to get long-term buy-in and avoid a household coup by sharing what you're learning (in an age-appropriate way, of course) with the children in your life and hearing their feedback on the matter. These conversations can help you gauge readiness for change and understand potential hurdles you'll want to address to keep the family united during a time of change. Talking it out helps reinforce your specific goals and also supports integrating what you're learning into something that eventually feels second nature. It's muscle memory. Just keep training, keep showing up, and know you've got a big ol' crowd rooting for you.

As my best friend Alexandria always says, "I'm waving my foam finger for ya!"

Chapter 1

PRIMED FOR CHANGE

When it comes to our kids, most parents will do whatever it takes to protect them. The tricky part becomes identifying threats that go undetected because they seem normal. Salient hazards don't elicit a protective response if we're unaware of their harm, desensitized to them or presuming innocence. The aim of this book isn't to scare (though some of this is enough to keep us up at night), but rather to slow our roll so we can spot the subtle signs of danger ahead. Intervening against the norm takes a lot more than just awareness, though I will certainly do my best to ensure this stuff is on our radar. It also takes will. It takes strategy (we'll get to that too). And it requires a holistic rethinking of how we proceed, resisting assumptions of safety and the push toward typical. It's like putting on 3-D glasses and suddenly everything comes right into focus. Getting comfortable with these new lenses, with changing your viewpoint, and with challenging beliefs is paramount to paving strategic, everyday zones for your family, and it begins with you picking up this book. Let's do this!

GETTING COMFORTABLE WITH UNCOMFORTABLE

I suppose it's not unusual to start to question a lot of things once you become a parent. This is familiar territory for me, as I am quite adept at changing my mind. I was a vegetarian for seventeen years before resuming meat with reckless abandon. I used to identify as a feminist liberal, and now... well, I increasingly relate more to crotchety old ladies who complain about shorts being too short on young girls. (Seriously though, ladies, you've got nothing to prove!) I spent years avoiding my father, whom I now meet with a ton of grace and gratitude.

If you're wondering what any of this has to do with parenting, the short answer is: *everything*. One of the key skills necessary to parent well is a willingness to change. Just think about all the hilarious memes out there that highlight the many rules and regulations we thought we'd uphold before having kids, only to actually have said kids and realize a lot of that wouldn't hold up. Said another way, we all think we're awesome parents... until we have kids.

Changing our minds, our patterns, our preconceived notions about how things will go in the future, is absolutely necessary for growth. As organizational psychologist and one of my personal favorite authors, Adam Grant, posted on X (that used to be Twitter to us old folks), "Refusing to change your mind is a decision to stop learning." And no one feels more like they're cramming the night before a massive test like a new parent, especially those of us who didn't spend a lot of time around kids before having our own. (The first diaper I ever changed was that of my firstborn, so I was a total newbie.)

Changing your mind isn't important only when first becoming a parent. It's a necessity throughout the journey, accommodating the seasons and shifts that come when children broach the various stages of childhood into adulthood. If we cling too tightly to the very same expectations that we hold about our children when they're approaching puberty as we did when they were newborns, we likely aren't giving our children the grace they need to unfold into who they were created to be.

What follows in this book isn't a How-To guide for parenting, per se. Instead, we are going to explore together some of the research and commentary that has emerged in the last dozen or so years that should absolutely be on our radar. The last thing most busy parents have time for—while navigating playdates, homework, endless runny noses, and meal planning—is keeping up with child development and neuroscience studies.

And it's probably not a surprise that much of the infrastructure that we trust to care for our children—looking at you, healthcare and public education—are simply too big and bureaucratic to respond quickly enough to emerging insights and best practices. My goal is to show parent and non-parent alike many of the most current trends and recommendations that can benefit our children, families, and communities. Allow me to be your nerdy little sherpa, if you will.

Beyond that, we're going to act. Not only will we learn why our observations about children are appropriately concerning, but we'll target exactly how to reverse negative trends and ensure our children stay on the narrow road toward thriving. Much of this work takes place in our homes, so we'll establish some new norms for your household.

As behavior-changing expert James Clear explains in his bestseller *Atomic Habits*, "The. . . idea is to create an environment where doing the right thing is as easy as possible. Much of the battle of building better habits comes down to finding ways to reduce the friction associated with our good habits and increase the friction associated with our bad one."

We'll get specific about how and where to increase or decrease friction to support our desired ends. Practical action steps are vital on the road of parenting, so there will be plenty of those mixed in with oodles of encouragement from a fellow rebel. I guess you can consider me part sherpa, part cheerleader.

The aim of this mentality shift is never to shame or belittle you, your children, or your choices. (The bossy, big-sister tone is very real, though. I come by it honestly.) I do ask you to come on this journey with an open mind, an open heart, maybe a highlighter in tow, and a *ton* of grace for yourself and your partner (and probably your parents, too). We don't know what we don't know, but we have an opportunity to change, to grow and do the hard thing, to hold each other accountable with humility, and to do it for the very best reason: our kids.

ESTABLISHING THE PARENTING ROLE

Ready for me to hit you with a culturally unpopular opinion? I hope so, because I imagine this may be the first of many. But to be fair, you didn't sign up for the status quo when you opened this book.

When I use the word "parent," I mean just that: an adult legally and ethically responsible for raising a child, biological or otherwise. I may also use the term "caregiver" to refer to grandparents, aunts/uncles, babysitters/nannies, teachers, children's ministry staff, and anyone else who is entrusted to care for someone else's child for any period of time. You will not, at any point, however, hear me use the term "friend" when referring to someone caring for a minor, especially when we're talking about parents.

Mom/Dad, you're not your child's friend. You are not their peer. You are a source of warmth, safety, and strength, and cultivating a strong attachment with your child is our life's sacred work. Friendships are beautiful and should absolutely be encouraged and cultivated in your child's life, but for any of this to play out well, you have to position yourself as a specific, unique person in your child's life. They may have many friends, but they have room for one mom, one dad. (Stepparents, you have a seat at the table here too, and a very important one. But you're not a friend either. Don't try to be.) Until they are of age, you're the navigator, and you have a vital role to play in their development in terms of what you do, but also what you *don't* do. Own that role and take it as seriously as you should.

The closer your children get to their adolescent years, the more distinctive your role and influence in your kid's life needs to be. Where peers are fickle and intense, you are steady and mature. Where friends form half-baked alliances, and drop them almost as quickly as they're made, your ability to show up consistently for your child never wavers. In a culture of superficiality and frivolity, let your home be a haven of depth where each is known and valued fiercely. Don't be a peer. Peers sometimes suck. Be the parent. As cultural critic Neil Postman puts it, "If parents wish to preserve childhood for their own children, they must conceive of parenting as an act of rebellion against culture."

If you're already in the friend zone, all is not lost. But you've got to remedy that. Expect pushback, and be ready to say many firm but loving "nos." Check out the inspiring and practical work of Gordon Neufeld, Gabor Maté, and Leonard Sax to help you course-correct. (Drs. Neufeld and Maté's *Hold On to Your Kids* and Dr. Sax's *The Collapse of Parenting* have been transformational in my own parenting.)

Your kids need you to assume your role as the parent to flourish and develop. If you're not up to speed on how children's brains function—spoiler alert: They're not fully developed until the mid-twenties—and what they need for proper physical and emotional development, read (or re-read) *The Whole Brain Child* by Drs. Daniel Siegel and Tina Payne Bryson. (Their book *No Drama Discipline* is also a gem, especially if you have some resetting of expectations and behavior management ahead of you.)

If you don't establish a relationship with your child in which you are leading the way—lovingly and humbly, of course—then nothing I'm about to share with you will make a modicum of difference in your child's life. You have to establish a position of influence and continuously cultivate it. What we're going to cover is exactly the kind of advocacy and coaching you want to impart in your children for life... not only for their own good, but for their children, and so on.

IT TAKES TWO

If you are raising kids with a partner, creating the zones we discuss will be a heck of a lot easier if you are both on board with the goal as well as the approach to get there. Establishing momentum and gaining traction are at risk if you have someone in an authority role in your home who is clearly not on board.

So one of the first steps I recommend is to have a chat with your person. If they're willing to read this book with you, even better! But many of us don't have partners who learn the same way we do. In that case, print a copy of the *Get in the Zone* tips in each chapter, share the social media profile of a prominent voice in a given zone to help "grease the wheels," or strike up conversations to convey the main points that resonate in your own words.

Generally, if it matters to you, it matters to your partner. But don't just start instituting change without providing some context. That goes for both your partner and your children.

There is a hilarious moment in the *Bluey* episode called "Faceytalk" (Season 3, episode 24) in which Uncle Stripe and Aunt Trixie are arguing about how to discipline the ever-challenging Muffin, cousin to Bluey and Bingo, who is once again defying her parent's instruction (in this case, to share the tablet with her little brother). Stripe threatens a time-out for Muffin, which Trixie quickly points out that they don't do anymore because "I read a book." Don't be like Aunt Trixie, folks. Please don't read this book and start implementing change to everyone's surprise, especially your spouse. It undermines you both.

Each zone we're targeting has very good reasons for pursuing, but you'll be hard-pressed to realize the fruits of your labor if you lead without sharing the insights that inspired you to make the changes in the first place. Take your family on the journey with you, and your impact will be far more powerful and lasting.

GET IN THE ZONE

- Embrace change and give yourself permission to change your mind (and your behaviors)
- Learn better, do better
- Reinforce (or establish) your role as the parent
- Bring your partner alongside you
- Practice articulating what you're learning to make it stick

CROSSING GUARDS

- Adam Grant — *Think Again: The Power of Knowing What You Don't Know*
- Daniel Siegel, MD and Tina Payne Bryson, PhD — *The Whole Brain Child: 12 Revolutionary Strategies to Nurture Your Child's Developing Mind*
- Daniel Siegel, MD and Tina Payne Bryson, PhD — *No Drama Discipline: The Whole-Brain Way to Calm the Chaos and Nurture Your Child's Developing Mind*
- Gordon Neufeld, PhD and Gabor Maté, MD — *Hold On to Your Kids: Why Parents Need to Matter More Than Peers*
- James Clear — *Atomic Habits: An Easy & Proven Way to Build Good Habits & Break Bad Ones*
- Leonard Sax, MD, PhD — *The Collapse of Parenting: How We Hurt Our Kids When We Treat Them Like Grown-Ups*
- William Stixrud, PhD and Ned Johnson — *The Self-Driven Child: The Science and Sense of Giving Your Kids More Control Over Their Lives*

Chapter 2

FOOD IS FUEL

Bold strategy, starting with food, eh? I didn't say this would be easy. But I promise it will be worth it. So let's tear off the wrapper, y'all!

PUT YOUR OXYGEN MASK ON FIRST

If you have a history of an eating disorder or a challenging history with food, I urge you to pursue some healing in this area before you broach this zone with your family. Whether you grew up poor with very little to eat, were left unchecked to overeat, or engaged in bulimia, the food journey with your child may be very triggering. You deserve help and healing when it comes to food and weight. One of the incredible blessings of children is that they sometimes force us to do the work in areas we'd prefer to avoid or repress, and in doing so, we find freedom.

You are not going to be able to show up well at the table if you are still carrying the weight (literally or figuratively) of disordered eating. Choose another zone to start with, but take the steps forward to get the help you need to restore your sense of safety in your body and to appreciate the role that food can and should play in your own health and well-being. Reach out to NEDA (the National Eating Disorder Association) and find a resource that can serve you.

IT'S WORTH THE (FOOD) FIGHT

Heaven knows there are many voices out there today decrying this food and that food, this ingredient and that, this *color* and those others, too. Advice is often conflicted, sources can be sketchy, fervor is intense, and meanwhile, you're doing your best to move beyond nuggets and mac-and-cheese on the menu 24/7. The struggle is so real. But it is important that we don't throw the baby out with the bathwater in this conversation. (I can't promise I won't use that metaphor again.)

The confusion and chatter surrounding food, especially when it comes to children, shouldn't scare us away from trying to make better choices. Remember, we're pushing back against the status quo, and the "comfortable" norm isn't serving any of us. Food isn't neutral. I am going to do my absolute best here to use the same kind of language we use in our own home to avoid labeling food as "good" or "bad." But I will not in any way perpetuate the lie that all food is the same.

By now it should not come as a surprise that many of the food products we see on our grocery store shelves are not actually fuel for our bodies. They are better categorized as entertainment which you happen to consume with your mouth. Calling them food is a travesty, but there are many well-meaning parents and caregivers who assume items on the shelf are safe. And in the sense that they won't *immediately* cause you bodily harm, they're considered acceptable for selling. But we should absolutely insist on a better criterion than that, especially when outcomes have shown us that disease is inevitable when subsisting on these non-nutritive products.

LITTLE BODIES, BIG IMPACTS

Children are disproportionately impacted by terrible nutrition. Sure, they've got youth on their side, but we can't overcome a terrible diet with a fantastic metabolism forever. Pediatric patients increasingly require the types of specialties and interventions that were previously reserved for adults and the elderly. Youth isn't what it used to be.

The Centers for Disease Control and National Institute of Health report that one in five children and adolescents in the United States are obese. Not overweight; obese. Up to 40 percent of obese children also suffer from non-alcoholic fatty liver disease (NAFLD), which can lead to liver failure and increases the risk of cardiovascular disease. In the general population of children (not just those who are obese), the prevalence of NAFLD is on par with asthma, up to 10 percent.

I harp on obesity and NAFLD because these diseases are absolutely preventable. In practice, this is one of the few areas where you will actually see conventional physicians discussing dietary modifications, even if not the most informed recommendations given their limited training and outdated sources. These conditions are also directly associated with food consumption. And while quantity is certainly a concern here, so is quality. Just because a child isn't bingeing on Cheetos and sodas by the case, that doesn't mean he's in the clear.

Food products that are loaded with added sugar, dyes, disruptive "fortified" ingredients, and inflammatory oils not only contribute to chronic overnutrition—consuming more calories than the body needs to function for sustained periods of time—but they also damage a young child's gut health.

And get this: Impaired gut health (known as "dysbiosis") is associated with increased risk of obesity! It's a vicious cycle, and it's up to us to help our babies get off this hamster wheel of bad health. As metabolic expert and functional health provider Dr. Casey Means asserts in *Good Energy*, "The world kids live in is inflammatory and metabolically disastrous unless parents staunchly go against the tide of 'normal' American culture."

Not only can this imbalance trigger a cascade of diseases, including autoimmune and chronic conditions, but it also impairs their immune system almost immediately. If nothing else, let the notion that cold and flu season might just be overconsumption-of-crap season—and therefore preventable—inspire you to lean in here.

WE KNOW BETTER

At the time of this writing, RFK's *Make America Healthy Again* movement is garnering plenty of attention in light of the 2024 presidential election. It's telling to see health—namely nutrition and food—so explicitly on the docket for someone pursuing a seat at the table in the White House, and to see incredible support for these efforts. What is surprising and encouraging is that this support seems to traverse party lines. Even many who don't favor RFK's endorsed candidate are willing to acknowledge that a healthier America would be pretty sweet.

We're also seeing a grassroots indictment on Kellogg's, led by food activist Vani Hari (a.k.a. "Food Babe"), with hundreds of thousands of people signing a petition to demand that the US-based company offer Americans the same, safer products that they sell in Europe, free from dyes and BHT. The brand is also being called out for explicitly marketing their sugary, dye-laden products to children, a practice that is shockingly not considered illegal (yet).

If you're wondering why food and health are discussed in tandem in these conversations, it's because we have data coming out our ears to assert that what you eat absolutely affects how you feel. And we have for decades.

Concern about the safety of products like ultraprocessed foods ("UPFs") have existed for many years. And you may be dismayed to learn how long there have been studies demonstrating risks—even before correlation and causation were determined— that should have warranted a pause, at a minimum. Instead, the food industry has grown. Exploded, really. And it has done so largely unchecked by the entities we assume are overseeing it.

Since most allopathic doctors take little to no courses in nutrition during their training, and given that it's still not uncommon for providers to tell us that diet and lifestyle won't improve our condition, we have to intervene on a microlevel (i.e., in our households) to forge a new path ahead. If we're waiting for the food industries and medical models to oblige and correct course, we're going to find ourselves and our families collateral damage.

No one will advocate for you and your family like you will. No politician, no executive, no lunch lady... no one is going to steward your family as well as *you* can.

Now that you know (or are reminded) of the problem at hand, and have a few startling examples of why this matters so much for children, let's get practical and think about how we can establish a zone for the young ones we love when it comes to what we eat.

FOOD LANGUAGE

How we talk about something with children can have a tremendous impact on how they retain what they've learned, as well as what connotations they have for the subject at hand. As parents and caregivers, we have the challenging job of striking a balance between age-appropriate honesty and coaching from a place of desire and bias. Bias gets a bad rap, but it isn't always such a bad thing. The key is to be aware of it and to get on top of any unhealthy associations you carry so that you don't pass those on to your kids. Many of us come into mealtimes with a little baggage, be it a history of eating disorder, poverty, tension at mealtimes, undiagnosed food allergies, or something else. We have to acknowledge these lingering associations in order to overcome them for the sake of our families.

When I was a young girl, we couldn't leave the dinner table until we were excused, which happened only after every bite of food was eaten off the plate. One of the regular items in rotation in our home was fresh fish. My dad was a seasoned fisherman and so we had freezers full of freshly caught tuna, dorado, swordfish, shark, you name it.

Unfortunately for my dad, his children didn't exactly appreciate the catch of the day. My mother was tasked with presenting palatable ways of serving the varieties of fish on hand to a hostile audience, the most successful of which was covering the fillets in cornflakes and frying them in Crisco, served with a side of ketchup. I don't know who had it worse: the kids, my dad, or the fish drowned in ketchup. Needless to say, mealtimes were tense when I was growing up.

Admonitions about "healthy" food were served up with a steaming hot side of guilt and moralized preference. I don't blame my folks, as it was a typical expectation in the '80s and '90s to clean your plates and appreciate what you had, especially among those who came from a history of poverty.

But when orders are given without context or consideration, the message rarely sticks and rebellion is sure to follow. (My weapon of choice: vegetarianism.) Let's pursue a middle ground, somewhere between ruling the dinner table with an iron fist and becoming a short-order cook for each family member. But we've got to watch our mouths and acknowledge our biases.

My favorite word to use when talking to my own kids about food is "balance." I don't generally talk about healthy or unhealthy, good or bad, or label things as "treats." Those terms are highly subjective, and even my husband and I have varying definitions of what would constitute a treat. If we are mindful of our language—choosing words like "balance" and "fresh" versus "bad" or "healthy"—we will navigate this zone with more grace and intentionality and less potential baggage to pass on.

How you discuss food will inevitably inform how your children talk about food, especially when they're young. It's short-sighted coaching that would teach a child to call certain foods "poison," knowing that word might be hurled in the school cafeteria without awareness of food scarcity or an eating disorder for the child in possession of said alleged poison. Children tend to lack nuance and discretion when they're still developing, so don't put words in their mouths that you wouldn't want parroted explicitly to someone else.

Very young children can be encouraged to first describe foods by color, shape, or smell. Older children can start to identify some of the benefits of fruits and vegetables, or of dairy and grains. Bring your elementary-aged children with you to the grocery stores so that you can teach them to understand labels and certifications, such as organic and gluten-free. What do these mean? How are these items different from nearby items on the shelf? What are some reasons people wouldn't choose them? This is also a great, practical exercise that invites consideration for perspectives outside of your own, creating empathy for folks who may have less money, less access to certain foods, or less information. Have your kids bag the groceries, too. Make a game out of it!

The last note when it comes to food language is to get really comfortable with the word *no*. "No" is a full sentence. Until your children are old enough to buy their own groceries and prepare their own food, you get to call the shots, and you're going to have different standards than they do. (If you don't now, you will.)

When you change what and when you offer meals or snacks, you will likely get pushback. Anticipate it and be ready. Don't react, don't lecture. Simply respond with a calm "No," or "Not right now;

we'll eat at [x time]." By all means, listen for constructive feedback, but you don't need to entertain the "But Mooooooooms."

Even after years of implementing balanced choices and constantly refining those in our home, my four-year-old asked for a milkshake just the other morning. At 7:00 a.m. After chuckling to myself, I simply said, "No, honey," and she moved on.

When you consistently and calmly stick to your guns, you will still get the asks. It's only natural, and children are amazing boundary-pushers. (It actually serves a developmental purpose, so take it as a good sign, especially as they approach adolescence.) Just as you expect their attempts, they will come to expect your responses. It won't be pretty at first, but after a while, you can deter the bids for candy and morning milkshakes with minimal drama.

FRESH FOOD FIRST!

One of the most powerful steps you can take when it comes to assembling meals or snacks for children is to start building the plate from the fridge. Fresh, whole foods are going to be your power move every single meal. When I say whole foods, I am talking about products that don't require a label because they *are* the ingredient: apples, bell peppers, carrots, pears, grapes, potatoes, rice, bananas, etc. We should absolutely teach label-reading, but step one is to favor foods that don't require labels.

I am a night-before lunch-maker. I always have been. One of the reasons I do this is because I stack meal assembly in the evening (in this case, lunch and dinner) to make prep and clean up more efficient. If I'm slicing fresh carrots for a dinner side, I might as well toss a few in the lunchboxes for tomorrow's lunch. No need to dirty up another knife and cutting board to cut up an organic apple for lunch, too.

But the other reason that I make lunches the night before is that I can be really intentional about influencing my kids' nutritional balance for the following day while I am on top of my game. I don't know about y'all, but school mornings can get a little hectic. Even as an early riser who can assemble my iced coffee in a matter of minutes, I don't need to add any more activity before school that takes away from moving my kids through the rhythms of morning time. Short on time and stressed, I am going to be far more likely to grab processed convenience foods out of the pantry versus pulling out the knife and cutting board.

When pulling together any meal, try to pull the majority of the ingredients out of the fridge. Let your staples and the majority of your plate consist of fresh food—organic if you can swing it.

Another step to making this fresh-food-first approach easy peasy is to invest a little time after grocery shopping or swinging by the farmers' market to prepare your food for convenience. Grab some glass containers (plastic contains endocrine-disrupting chemicals, so leave those budding hormones alone), put on some great tunes, and have yourself a prep party. Slice up carrots, celery, and bell peppers in one container. Wash grapes and strawberries, dry them, and put them in easy-to-see containers in the fridge so you don't lose sight of what you have. Boil a handful of eggs for a quick, high-protein snack on the go. Cook some rice in bone broth with grass-fed butter for a nutrient-dense side that just needs warming. Buy heads of broccoli instead of pre-cut to save some cash, then cut and bag the florets for upcoming meals. (Bonus: this allows time for an enzyme called sulforaphane to activate, providing even more protective benefits if you consume within forty minutes of cutting. Prepped broccoli florets can last in the fridge for about four days.)

Rinse cherry tomatoes and keep the container on the counter to grab by the handful. No judgment if you snack as you prep!

When you have fresh food washed and ready to go, it makes assembling snacks between errands and last-minute-lunch-making incredibly easy, all while continuing to focus on whole foods. And since it's a party in here, grab the kids! Involving children in meal prep and food shopping encourages curiosity and fosters buy-in when it comes time to eating meals.

Picky-eating expert Jennifer Anderson of *kidseatincolor.com* calls these encounters "exposures," laying the no-pressure foundation for eventual exploration and enjoyment of new foods. As if that weren't motivation enough, participation in these activities also cultivates practical skills like making shopping lists, understanding ingredient labels, following recipes, and kitchen safety.

Leading with whole foods provides the added benefit of filling the majority of plates (and stomachs) with beneficial nutrients that we were biologically designed to consume. This establishes a firm nutritional foundation that can handle the occasional Oreo. It's all about balance. The 80/20 rule certainly applies here, so shoot for food that nourishes 80 percent of the time, and barring any major health concerns, you'll find that your kiddos can enjoy the 20 percent without the prevailing chronic disease path of their peers.

A SEAT AT THE TABLE

Today's busy schedules are not only exhausting, but they are actually antithetical to some of the best practices for family and individual flourishing. We'll cover this more in depth in Chapter 5, but given we're on the topic of food at the moment, we simply have to discuss the importance of communal family meals.

Slowing down for a family meal at the table with your kids is, whether you realize it or not, a radical push back to the on-the-go, every-man-for-himself dinnertime that is so prevalent in the US these days. Family members scattered through the house, eating different meals, phones occupying their minds while they chow down, is a typical picture for dinnertime.

But friends, let's not. While I am a huge fan of the occasional meal away from the table ("pizza picnics" on the living room floor while watching a movie are a favorite in the Gonzalez home), we can make headway in several zones by shooting for a majority of our dinners each week taking place together, at the dining table/bar/kitchen nook.

If visions of flawless tablescapes, fancy linens, and charger plates are flooding your mind at the moment, I want to assure you that most of us aren't that fancy. Sure, a gorgeous spread here and there can make anyone feel like a queen or king, but there is no bougie required to embody the spirit of hospitality, even for your own family. Shoot for a matching set of real plates and silverware, grab some fun, reusable napkins (I love my flannel, kid-friendly patterned cloth napkins from Etsy), and don't overthink it. If all you have to offer right now is paper plates and take-out napkins, go for it! Make it happen with what you have.

Family dinner is a means to several different, desirable ends, including protective benefits for your children. A study published in the *Journal of Adolescent Health* revealed, "The frequency of family dinner is an external developmental asset or protective factor that may curtail high-risk behaviors among youth." It went on to state, "Family rituals such as regular mealtimes may ease the stress of daily living in the fast-paced families of today's society."

Another 2004 study from the same journal examined the relationship between family meals and disordered eating and found that in general, frequent communal meals can also protect against unhealthy eating behaviors, especially in food-positive households like the ones we're cultivating with this zone. It can be tough out there, especially for young women, so bolstering our children's ability to endure rough seasons of adolescence via shared meals is an incredible parenting move.

Another benefit of family dinner with the kids is that it allows regular opportunities to connect with one another throughout the week. This only works if the screens are off and smartphones put away, mind you. (That includes you, Mom and Dad.) Like I mentioned, the occasional movie during dinner isn't going to detract from your efforts. But by setting the expectation that meal time is generally "unplugged," you'll create the kind of buffers that may be the critical opportunities you get during a busy week to make eye contact, catch up, or (most importantly) pick up on subtle clues that someone at the table has something on their mind.

At this point, we are definitely talking less about what is on the plate and more about a connection point with your kids. So while we absolutely target fresh, whole foods without a side of pressure, don't forget to save some steam for the actual shared experience ahead of you. This is the good stuff, and this can be transformational for your parenting journey, determining the kind of relationship and influence you have with your babies.

GIVING CANDY TO A BABY

At the onset of my daughter's fourth year, I thought we were finally coming out of the more challenging aspects of the toddler phase, ushering in the delight that is the preschool years.

We were seeing fewer meltdowns, less defiance, better articulation of feelings and needs, and a more balanced sense of self overall. It was incredible to see our little girl shine so brightly and to watch her unique personality unfold unfettered.

Then she started a new preschool.

We had relocated to a Fort Worth suburb in the past year to be closer to family. Given her social aptitude and demeanor, we didn't think much of switching her final year of preschool to one that was less than five minutes from our house. She was excited for the new school and new friends, and dove right in with nary a tear or protest. But after a few weeks of incessant worksheets, an introduction to homework, and a treat-based rewards system, things started to change in our contented little lady.

For every optional homework sheet she completed (yes, another worksheet), she received a Dum Dum lollipop as a reward. This became her driving motivation for practicing her letters and numbers.

Ostensibly this was not such a bad thing, but extrinsic motivation is seldom helpful, especially when it involves candy. (Bribery, I believe it's called.) A treasure box filled with candy and junky, small toys was available to reward other aspects of their preschool days as well, such as good behavior.

Dum Dums are tiny. I get it. The occasional piece of conventional candy doesn't make me lose sleep. (Remember our 80/20 goal? We got this.) But it wasn't the sugar that was the issue; it was the exposure. Suddenly having the presence of candy associated with school, as a reward for something, was disrupting our after-school rhythms every single day. And that's putting it mildly.

"Why don't I have a sucker in my folder today? But I did all my work. I thought it was a blue day, but my teacher said it was a green day. Please, Mommy, please can I have a suuuuckerrr."

First of all, I don't even know what a blue day versus a green day looks like. (I've asked. It's complicated.) Second, it's 2025. Why are other people feeding kids that aren't theirs? I understand that some schools provide lunches and snacks. Fine. But springing candy on parents without so much as a quick check to ensure we're on board? Absolutely not.

While this specific circumstance is unusual to some, I am constantly amazed by stories from friends and acquaintances describing how often food is offered to children without respect for parents' wishes or even consent. From playdates to rewards at school, to goodie bags and fundraiser swag, candy and non-nutritive food directed at kids abounds.

And here's the rub: My ability as a parent to enjoy that 20 percent we're targeting for balance and optimal habits is diminished when my girl has already devoured a birthday cupcake and sucker before 2 p.m. (The frequency of birthday treats outnumbers kids. Make it make sense.) I can't surprise her with an after-school ice cream at our favorite local ice cream shop with dye-free sprinkles and fresh whipped cream if she's already riding the sugar high of another day at preschool.

As parents and caregivers, it's wise to consider that we're always competing with flashy packaging and cutesy mascots that are enticing our children to consume. (That's playing dirty.) And in consuming, they develop the taste buds and appetite that crave only more high-sugar, highly processed food products. The Standard American Diet (SAD, indeed) favors UPFs, breeds food addiction, and (again) disproportionately impacts children. I'm not a conspiracy theorist, but it doesn't take much to discern that enticing young future consumers and getting them hooked on your product isn't exactly an accident.

Seeing school lunches filled with sugary snacks and processed foods can be really tough for kids who show up with the beautiful fresh-food-first bounty we assembled the night before. But given that kids also tend to try things when they're not at home, lunch time at school can also be an awesome opportunity for exposures.

The first time my daughter actually ate the small slice of cucumber served to her (as served many, many times before), it was in her school lunch. And do you know what the difference was on this particular lunch day? I cut the cucumber into the shape of a heart with one of those tiny food cutters from Amazon.

(Because we are competing with shiny crap, I am admittedly an advocate of some cute fruit picks and shape cutters.) You don't have to go full-blown Pinterest Mom, but a few fun touches here and there—especially if your kid struggles with variety and prefers the same things over and over again—may earn you some serious gains in the school cafeteria.

As more school lunches lead with fresh wholeness versus sugary packages/processing, our kids will have far less "FOMO" (fear of missing out). We can normalize real food for kids, and I truly believe we can change the cultural expectation that we have to bribe our children with junk to make them eat. Serve beautiful food, consistently, and get the kids involved, and we can transform our little eaters into fueled-up bodies that thrive.

TEENS AND TREATS

Teenagers are basically adults-on-the-brink. Sure, their brains still have another five to ten years before fully developed (and it sometimes shows), but our role in their lives inevitably starts to change the closer they get to leaving the nest. I don't, however, subscribe to the idea that teens and preteens are lost causes. They may very well be able to procure any manner of snacks and beverages that aren't preferable even for the 20 percent category of balance. The tough reality is you can't control that; you can't control them. But in my experience, teenagers are typically broke. They are increasingly driving later into their teens, as well. This means that you generally have a captive audience when they're home.

Blue Heat Takis may be the snack of choice when they're grabbing a snack from the vending machines at school. (Bless it, you don't even have to know about it.) But that doesn't mean it's provided at home. You continue to stay the course, keeping the fridge filled with fresh, ready-to-grab whole foods that nourish their bodies, and limit pantry snacks to those that avoid dyes and inflammatory oils and include ingredients that actually constitute fuel. Save sodas and sports drinks for special occasions, eating out, or... sports. Let them complain. Let them sulk away from the pantry, resigned. If they're hungry, they'll choose from what is available. Your job is to toe the line, normalize the 80 percent as the majority of their diet, and let the rest go.

Whether they like it or not, as they become adults and get into their own place, their expectations for what they see when they open the refrigerator or pantry door is a balanced variety of fuel that they'll eventually emulate, knowing it's the example you set of how we feed our bodies. Well done, friend.

EXPECT THE DETOX

Have you ever tried going a period of time without your morning coffee? Maybe you simply had to fast for lab work or a procedure and had to skip your cup of joe. Perhaps you've observed Lent or implemented a resolution to eliminate sweets or desserts. How'd that work out for you? If you're shamelessly heaped over a pan of brownies as you read this, let me remind you: You're in a safe place. Put the brownies down.

Many of us have our thing, our vice, our crutch that we'd be hard-pressed to give up, especially in the thick of momming and dadding. For me, it's my organic iced coffee with whole milk every morning. To be honest, I often feel better when I have to skip it for fasting labs, but I also love it. Like, love it, love it. Because most of us know how it feels to go without, we should approach this zone with a ton of compassion.

Our kids have even less willpower than we do, given that the executive functioning portion of the brain isn't online just yet. They literally cannot just decide to not miss candy and sweets. You can't and shouldn't expect them to nod in agreement when you implement some of the changes in the *Get in the Zone* section of this chapter (or any section, for that matter). They're not robots, and they're sure as heck not going to like it.

The more their diets consist of added sugar, processed ingredients, dyes, and inflammatory oils, the more dysregulated they are physically and mentally and the more addicted they are physiologically. Please expect pushback and expect a period of detox. Meltdowns may ensue, socks may be thrown, insults hurled, and you may very well land on the Worst Parent Ever list. (You're in good company.)

This is not about being popular. This journey is about providing the safest environment possible for your child to flourish and develop. So brace for the hard stuff, hold strong, and remember that you are not the only parent who has had to endure the saddest little cries (or rage-filled screams) over the absence of Skittles.

Solidarity, my friend.

A CASE STUDY WITH ZONE VIBES

There is an emerging awareness that I've been tracking that shows promise in terms of positive "food peer pressure." Food allergies in children have become a growing concern, with one in fifteen American kids suffering from some kind of food allergy. This equates to approximately two children per classroom, according to the Centers for Disease Control.

The proliferation of nut allergies, in particular, has changed many lunch-room policies given the severity of reaction for some kids. Churches and school staff are trained to administer Epi-Pens, and classrooms are now equipped with special utensils, cleaning supplies, and labels to ensure those allergic stay safe. Other parents are asked to refrain from sending peanuts to school to help protect affected children.

Allergy-aware spaces are giving zone vibes! To ensure the few with allergies are safe, the many are asked to refrain from bringing (or at least sharing) the offending ingredient to protect the vulnerable kiddos. While I'm not suggesting that schools regulate lunches, restricting candy, dyes, and processed snacks (that's not their job), it is a positive step in the direction of raising awareness that foods are not neutral. They can be damaging.

In light of this, perhaps more parents will recognize that what we pack in lunchboxes matters and will lean into whole foods and nutrient-dense products, foods that inherently keep little bodies from getting sick, balance blood sugar, and prevent hyperactivity when replacing added sugar and dyes. Imagine your kids not complaining about the lack of dye-infused chips and sugary muffins in *their* lunches because no one else has those either. Do you know what kids don't complain about cupcakes missing in their lunches? Kids who have never seen cupcakes in lunches.

We can start shifting the tides toward mealtimes that meet the true needs of growing bodies and avoid the pitfalls that land our kids on lifelong medication or in the doctor's office, one school lunch or prep party at a time.

FOOD AS A FOUNDATION

We are competing with an industry that makes billions of dollars by convincing folks they're too busy to cook and that switching to convenience food is a neutral shift. This hurtful ploy is costing millions of children their well-being and is disruptive to protective family rhythms. We make time for what matters to us, and especially in light of the sobering statistics about pediatric health that we covered in this chapter, I hope *this* matters to you.

This zone has significant return on investment because food as fuel is the foundation of our kids' whole bodies, minds, and emotions. What we feed them feeds *all* of them. Start here, and you'll give yourself a head start on everything else in this book. You can start small—make it sustainable—but start!

GET IN THE ZONE

- Acknowledge that food isn't neutral
- Be mindful of your language when discussing food
- Seek help for food baggage before implementing this zone
- Load up on fresh, whole foods first for every meal
- Shoot for variety (even different color apples or grapes represent variety—eat the rainbow)
- Choose organic whenever possible
- Avoid dyes and added sugar (READ THE LABELS)
- Involve your children in meal prep and grocery shopping
- Toe the line and keep offerings at home aligned with the 80 percent goal

CROSSING GUARDS

- B. Brett Finlay, PhD and Marie-Claire Arrieta, PhD — *Let Them Eat Dirt: Saving Your Child from an Oversanitized World*
- Be Well By Kelly (Kelly LeVeque) — *https://bewellbykelly.com/*
- Casey Means, MD — *Good Energy: The Surprising Connection Between Metabolism and Limitless Health*
- Elisa Song, MD — *Healthy Kids, Happy Kids: An Integrative Pediatrician's Guide to Whole Child Resilience*
- Feeding Littles (Megan McNamee, MPH, RDN) — *https://feedinglittles.com/*

- Just Ingredients (Karalynne Call) — *https://justingredients.us/*
- Kids Eat In Color (Jennifer Anderson, RD) — *https://kidseatincolor.com/*
- Leonardo Trasande, MD, MPP — *Sicker, Fatter, Poorer: The Urgent Threat of Hormone-Disrupting Chemicals to Our Health and Future... And What We Can Do About It*
- National Eating Disorders Association — *https://www.nationaleatingdisorders.org/get-help/*

Chapter 3

SUPERPOWERED SLEEP

F ew topics elicit groans from parents like that of sleep. A 2022 Gallup Survey reveals that about fifty to seventy million Americans have sleep disorders. So not even tying the subject to children, almost a third of us are on the struggle bus when it comes to sleep. Adding children and their sleep needs and challenges to the conversation... we're tired even thinking about it.

Recognizing the important role of sleep for our overall health, the US Department of Health and Human Services set as one of their Healthy People 2023 objectives to increase the proportion of children who get sufficient sleep relative to their age. Optimal sleep quantities vary, but generally eight to fourteen hours (including naps) is the norm for kids. The objective states, "Not getting enough sleep is linked to heart problems, obesity, and diabetes — and it can affect concentration, learning, mood, and behavior." If you're thinking, *That'll preach*, you're not alone, as many of us have felt these impacts in our own bodies. What's concerning about this particular measure is that there has been little improvement since data collection began in 2016. Where the goal is over 70 percent of children getting sufficient sleep, we're still hovering close to 65 percent, which is where the data started.

In other words, we're not improving our children's ability to get sufficient sleep at the national level. And this is a problem. Not only for them, but for us, too. And I'm not just talking about groggy mornings and evening meltdowns. Our ability to encourage our children toward healthier choices and behaviors is going to be limited if we're dealing with a little body that is not getting basic needs met. Just as we discussed the importance of proper fuel in Chapter 2, making headway with an exhausted child is no more effective than working with a "hangry" one.

We must, as parents, counteract the hustle culture that threatens even our youngest members of society, encouraging hours of school, homework to boot, and a plethora of extracurricular activities that keeps the candle burning from first dawn until after dark. (We'll hit this dynamic hard in Chapter 5.)

We cannot expect children to perform and grow as needed if a satisfactory sleep zone isn't in place, nor can we simply look for midday yawns or "Witching Hour" meltdowns to signal whether they are getting sufficient sleep. The signs can be much more subtle: declining grades, waning interest in social activities or extracurriculars, changes in eating habits, difficulty remembering things, short temper, lack of motivation. I don't know about you, but I could place most teens and preteens that I know in this list at least in part, if not fully. Maybe it's not a generational problem. Maybe they're freaking exhausted.

Waiting for negative manifestations of lack of sleep is a bad move. Let's get out of a reactive stance and get more proactive with it. Just as we shouldn't wait for our bodies to get sick to slow down, prioritization of sleep and rest are paramount for children who are actively growing and changing in ways we can't even fathom.

If you read *The Wonder Weeks* by Hetty van d Rijt, Xaviera Plooij, and Frans D. Plooij, you're already aware of the sheer volume of activity underway every few weeks in an infant's development. For those who haven't read *The Wonder Weeks*, the book tracks what the authors call "Leaps," developmentally-dependable stages that children pass through, marked by predictable behaviors or manifestations aligned with the nature of the Leap. The book covers newborn through age two, but I'll be honest, I could use "The Wonder Years" through the mid-twenties to understand just what the heck is going on behind the curtain.

We can't see everything going on, nor can children articulate their feelings and shifts, but it's substantial and it's constant. They must rest along the way. According to the Mayo Clinic, "Sleep is a crucial biological function. Loss of sleep is hypothesized to play a significant role in restoring and recovering the body systems, learning, memory consolidation and healthy brain development.

Sleep deprivation can lead to physical and behavioral symptoms that can be misdiagnosed as more severe mental and behavioral disorders." When mental and behavioral disorders for children are on the rise, we cannot continue to ignore this vital pillar of health, even when the cultural pace does so.

A study published in 2021 indicated a 34.6 percent increase in the prevalence of mental illness in children aged four to seventeen. That number has only grown since the pandemic, and the lasting effects of this disruption for this generation will likely continue to unfold in decades to come.

I am not saying that we can counteract the effects of a global pandemic with sleep, but I am absolutely saying that getting better sleep improves recovery, resilience, and immune health. We can't predict the future or put our kids in bubble wrap, but we can sure as heck ensure that in our homes, sleep is prioritized and sacred.

Did you know that studies have demonstrated that moderate sleep deprivation results in impairments similar to that of alcohol intoxication? I don't have to even ask if you would let your child attend school, drive, or otherwise try to function while under the influence. Knowing what we know now, the impairment is very real. We cannot sleep on prioritizing sleep another night. (I couldn't resist.) No more snoozing on this crucial zone! (OK, I promise I'll stop.)

PERMISSION TO SLEEP FREELY

My sleep journey with my first, my son Asher, was incredibly difficult. He was a lean baby, which meant constant feeding (coupled with a bad latch), and he didn't seem to follow any of the expectations I had when it came to sleep. All the parenting books I had read talked about several-hours stretches of sleep and sleeping independently, and those were nowhere to be found for us. A decent stretch for us was a single, whole hour.

I felt like a failure as a mother, and I was sure my kid was somehow broken. Sleep training was a total bust, even with a very expensive sleep coach. I held or wore him for every single nap, and every time I had to enter into a sleep cycle (basically every few hours with an infant), I felt my body tense as I held back tears.

Here's what really threw me: "Drowsy but awake" never led to sleep for us. "Cry it out" didn't result in solid sleep either. The go-to methods for getting newborns to sleep weren't working.

I eventually understood that expecting a three-month-old to do anything independently is fundamentally unfair. Parents, we've been lied to. We've been told that the only healthy, safe way to sleep is according to many rules that counter every biological desire and instinct in our bodies. Yes, sleep deprivation risk is real. Yes, we must consider the well-being of Mom and Dad. But the idea that optimal baby sleep and meeting parental needs are mutually exclusive is a big, fat (sleep) sack of crap.

Do you want to know when my own sleep went from sad to super? When I had my daughter. Yes, on the heels of having a newborn, I discovered the best sleep rhythms of my life. I threw those cultural instructions out the window, attuned to my baby, and I leaned in. I gladly held her for every nap, welcoming the chance to rest my very busy mind and body. (It's almost like a new mother needs rest too. Weird.)

I snuggled her to sleep next to me every night, observing safe co-sleeping practices with nary a concern for what others said I should (or should not) be doing. I followed her cues and discovered a consistent circadian rhythm that, yes, meant waking early even on the weekends, but that yielded quantities of deep sleep and Rapid Eye Movement (REM) sleep that I didn't have in my teens and twenties as a troubled sleeper.

There is plenty of information out there when it comes to how kids sleep, and I am certainly no expert here, but I can tell you from the bottom of my heart that most of our cultural mores around sleep are misguided. They do not honor nor reflect the centuries of parenting traditions or biological norms for the mother-child dyad. If you feel like you're doing it wrong, you're probably just listening to the wrong voices.

A survey by The Lullaby Trust, a European sleep advocacy organization for babies and children, reported that nine in ten parents co-slept with their baby. I intentionally cite a European resource here given the US is still heavily biased toward crib-sleep, and therefore I doubt most parents feel comfortable admitting to American pediatricians when they are "breaking the rules" by bed sharing. The point is, there is no one-size-fits-all for how any family sleeps. What's key is that we yield for this zone to ensure it's prioritized.

Sleep transformed for me and my family when I got off the internet and gave myself permission to listen to my instincts as a mother. And this isn't just for the infant stage. I still feel no guilt or frustration when my now eight-year-old needs support getting his restless mind to quiet. Just tonight, I rocked my four-year-old to sleep in the same recliner that has seen hours of contact naps. These are *children*. Nighttime represents extended hours of separation and darkness. How can we possibly judge young minds and hearts for wanting connection from their attachment figures before falling asleep?

To allay some of the inevitable fears in this area, I am happy to report that my kids are incredible sleepers. I still lie with them to help my daughter fall asleep (generally a ten-minute task), and they share a bedroom for sleep (and will do so as long as they'll tolerate it). Co-sleeping and breaking the rules didn't break them, didn't doom them to sleeping with Mommy forever. They still occasionally wake at night needing the restroom, water, or a cuddle after a bad dream. *As do I.* Let's ensure that our expectations of our children and their sleep account for the fact that they're humans—not pets, not machines.

(If you're in the throes of teething, regression, or anything else disturbing your sweet cherub's sleep, it's perfectly natural that you want to punch me in the face right now. But hold fast to this: The nights are long, but the days are short. Pretty soon, they'll be too big to rock. And I am not ashamed to admit that I'll be a little brokenhearted.)

You may need different rhythms to find a sustainable solution for your family, but this zone requires giving yourself permission to reject the one-size-fits-all pressures around childhood sleep.

SETTING THE STAGE FOR SLEEP

It's incredible to think of how little most pediatricians and parenting books talk about sleep hygiene. We've all heard "Get plenty of sleep," but without practical action steps, that instruction is about as helpful as saying "Stay healthy." OK, but *how*?

If the term "sleep hygiene" is new to you, this is basically a set of practices that helps your body prepare for and enter into a great night of sleep. We need to consider the behaviors and the environment we cultivate for our children to inspire solid slumber and promote optimal recovery.

Anecdotally I've found that many parents insist they have good sleep practices for their home, but when we run through the list, they come up short. I don't blame parents; I blame the lack of conversation around the importance of sleep and practical changes we can implement based on sleep science to cultivate the best sleep possible.

The following sections include some of the action steps we can take toward cultivating a strong sleep zone for your family, bearing in mind that these provide cumulative benefits. The more we do, the better it works!

CONSISTENT SLEEP AND WAKE SCHEDULE

Wait, am I actually suggesting waking early on the weekend? If you have small children, you are probably laughing at the mere idea of that being a choice. (It's not.) When children are young and healthy, their body clocks are actually incredibly precise. You could set the oven clock by their schedules.

When people suggest that keeping a child up later will help them sleep in, my husband and I have a good laugh. This is one of their super powers, honestly, and adults would do well to emulate their sleep patterns to experience the benefit of a well-tuned circadian rhythm. Turning in and waking up at the same time every day can do wonders for optimizing your sleep... as well as the rest of your day.

Circadian rhythms are discussed often when it comes to sleep, but these cycles actually impact far more than catching our Zs. Hormone fluctuations, appetite, body temperature, mood, and sleep are all associated with an individual's cycle. Our circadian rhythms can adapt over time, which is actually great news if your current cycle is suboptimal. But one of the keys for establishing a healthy rhythm is *consistency*.

I own an Oura ring and love how this handy tool helps me monitor all my health and wellness data, including sleep data, throughout my days and nights. (Nerd alert.) One of the metrics used to evaluate the sleep score is "Timing." This data point takes into consideration total sleep, midpoint of overnight sleep, and how those align with your individual chronotype, which is that natural inclination toward "morning person" or "night owl."

When I stay up late to watch another episode of *Frasier* that I've already seen fifteen times before, I take a hit on my timing measurement. I have an optimal bedtime based on my average sleep over time, and the later I go past that window, the lower my score will go, because there is no sleeping in. Not because I have young children (who will miraculously play quietly until there are signs of life from Mommy and Daddy's room), but because my body's clock knows when it's 6:45 a.m. Alarm or not, I'm awake.

If your goal is to establish a new rhythm, be it going to sleep earlier or waking earlier (or even later), give your body some time to adjust. We can't turn our training on a dime, just as you can't suddenly lift one-hundred pounds at the gym when you've been hanging out with the fifteen-pounder.

The same is true for our children. If you decide to shift bedtime earlier to avoid the preschool grumps, don't expect your babes to magically turn in with nary a complaint or wiggle on day one. It will take time, but you'll get there.

Timing is important in terms of pre-midnight snoozing, too. As neurobiologist and sleep specialist Dr. Allison Brager told *Fortune*, going to sleep before midnight is essential to optimize REM sleep. REM sleep is associated with learning and memory, so this stage of sleep is critical for children and can have a direct impact on their performance in school, at their jobs, or even around the house.

I have personally experienced that it is also very difficult to get decent levels of deep sleep after midnight, which is crucial for healing, immune system function, hormone regulation, and tissue, bone, and muscle repair.

In other words, if you expect your child to be healthy—mind, body, and spirit—without a consistent sleep schedule that starts before midnight, it's not going to happen. Help them understand the importance of sleep, why it matters for their bodies (now and in the long run), and what the goal is for a new sleep schedule. This insight and training will benefit them as adults, too, so it's invaluable to intervene now. And don't ask them to do anything you're not going to do yourself. Kids learn best via modeling, and you can bet your instruction will ring shallow if they see the light glowing under your bedroom door well into the early morning hours. Not to mention, you're going to need some rest to do this parenting work well. Get your dream on!

KITCHEN CLOSED BEFORE BED

I hope that Chapter 2 shed some light on the importance of diet when it comes to well-being. Yet another implication of what we eat and drink is how it impacts our sleep. Establishing an ideal bedtime based on the previous section in this chapter is a great reference point to back into how you want to structure your meals and beverages to support desired sleep timing.

Caffeine is a well-established killer of solid snoozing. Given our culture's obsession with hustle, however, I don't think we are quite serious enough about when we need to put the cuppa down. A good rule of thumb is to avoid caffeine-containing products—which can be foods and beverages, so check the label—after noon. The earlier we can consume and wrap up caffeine, the better, but noon should be the cut off. If we imbibe in the afternoon, we can expect sleep to take a hit.

For children, caffeine should be a no-go. This isn't a judgy mom perspective. The American Academy of Child and Adolescent Psychiatry (AACAP) put out a statement in 2020 asserting, "There is no proven safe dose of caffeine for children." Yes, many kids in middle school/junior high and high school are dragging their sleepy bodies to the morning bell with Red Bull, Prime Energy, soda, or

Venti Frappuccinos. Again, you're the parent. And your teens are probably broke. Don't provide it, don't pay for it.

If we're going to curb the caffeine, we must encourage good sleep habits and balanced support when they're struggling and feel like they need a boost. Hot herbal tea in the morning with a little manuka honey and lemon for immune support may satisfy the desire to have something in their hand on the way to school. Slice lemons and limes to add to their stainless to-go bottle if they're bored with plain water. And a protein-rich breakfast can go a long way toward regulating blood sugar and giving their bodies fuel for the day.

Speaking of blood sugar, eating within two hours of bedtime is also going to make it difficult to hit those sleep goals. Bodies need time to digest, and if your children's blood sugar is spiking as they crawl into bed, that's going to undermine your efforts. Shoot for earlier dinner times, limit after-dinner snacks, and keep an eye on the clock. We don't have to be militant here, but we can't serve our kids late-night sugar bombs and wonder why they just won't settle in. A walk around the block after dinner is also a great way to help regulate blood sugar, reduce bloating, and help dinner settle well before bedtime.

BUSY UNTIL BEDTIME

I'm reminded in talking about circadian rhythms that many families are basically busy right up until bedtime. Between homework, errands, extracurriculars, and sports, you may already feel defeated trying to back into a solid sleep schedule. Even with the sweetest nighttime routine, if your kid is coming in hot and wired, it's going to go south. I mean, have you ever tried calmly singing "You Are My Sunshine" to a child hanging from the top bunk like a wild ape? It's not the vibe.

Let me lovingly remind you that you don't have to do all of this. I'm jumping ahead a bit to Chapter 5, but it's worth repeating that many kids would do well with less on their plate, schedule-wise. And your family's needs matter too, so if something you're doing for your children isn't serving the goals you're trying to set for your family, that is worth a conversation.

Don't buy into the lie of keeping up with the Joneses, thinking this is required to keep your child competitive, on track, or enriched. The best things for young brains and bodies are really quite simple. (Kim John Payne and Lisa M. Ross's *Simplicity Parenting* is a must-read on this front.)

Imagine how you and your children will stand out when they're rested, grounded, connected, and well enough to meet the day and its challenges fully equipped. This zone can draw attention from miles away when done well—and what an incredible way to encourage others with your example. Remember: We want to reroute norms, and this kind of positive influence is incredibly powerful.

LIGHT THE WAY

We're going to touch briefly on devices here, but we won't hit this subject in depth until Chapter 4. (Gird your loins.) Nevertheless, screen time or smartphones in bed leading up to sleep is going to cause a major jam in this zone.

Dr. Ben Carter and his colleagues published an article in *JAMA* that revealed just how disruptive portable screen-based media devices are on various sleep metrics. Devices are ideally kept completely out of bedrooms in the evening, charged overnight in airplane mode in another room.

The alluring glow of our favorite apps may sound relaxing, but having the entirety of information via the internet at your fingertips as you try to unwind is antithetical to optimal sleep preparation. But as Dr. Carter asserts, "The most important point is that we need a communitywide strategy to empower parents so that it becomes an acceptable routine to remove devices prior to bedtime."

He's talking about a zone! We *all* need to react to these findings to reroute norms, pushing back against this cultural default. Instead, normalizing grabbing a book when winding down not only eliminates the late-night stimulation of smartphones in bed, but can actually improve sleep quality.

Device recommendations regarding sleep also highlight the impact of light on our sleep success. Given that most of us aren't farmers these days, the idea of waking and sleeping when the sun rises and sets isn't typical. But observing this light cycle throughout the day is actually really important for cultivating a strong circadian rhythm. Getting sunlight on your eyes within an hour of waking is a great way to kick-start your body's processes to encounter the day ready for action.

Establish a practice of walking the dog with your kids early in the morning, or share a cup of hot tea sitting on the front porch with sunlight in view. Have them practice their spelling words while hanging out on the backyard swing before school. Just give them a chance to get sunlight on their eyes to awaken their body and mind... and get some Vitamin D synthesizing while they're at it.

Similarly, limiting cool-toned lighting—especially blue light—before bed signals to our bodies that it's time to start winding down. This is key for melatonin production, which doesn't kick in if we're constantly exposed to bright lights such as the blue tones emitted by smartphones, tablets, and televisions. Melatonin is required for sleep, and simply supplementing with this hormone should not be the first line of defense when other sleep hygiene practices (such as those in this section) are ignored.

Our bodies are the best source for regulating our cycles, so help your children leverage their innate cues by limiting overhead lighting, playing outside at sunset, incorporating amber bulbs through the house for nighttime activities, and shutting down the screens at least a few hours before bed. If you do use devices before bed, grab some blue-light-blocking glasses and use night-mode filters on devices to reduce melatonin impairment.

Listen, I understand there are seasons when we leverage devices to keep our sanity. I get it. My husband travels a lot, and especially with two young kids, I understand how valuable that break can be. However, I've also experimented with watching movies right up until bedtime (with blue-light-blocking glasses, of course), and with having the kids play, read, or do games up until bedtime, and there is no contest which leads to quicker, drama-free bedtime. (It's the latter, if that's not obvious.)

As author and parent Andy Crouch asserts in *The Tech-Wise Family*, "Like almost all technology, illumination on demand—with technology's signature qualities, easy and everywhere—is in many ways a gift. But it is also a powerful nudge in the wrong direction, and as a result many of us are chronically deprived of sleep and its benefits." If your kids are accustomed to sliding into the evening with screens and shows, this zone may be challenging. But the sooner you establish expectations and encourage screen-free activities before bed, the sooner they'll pick up the habit and know that's the new norm.

Another aspect of the sleep environment we need to consider is how dark we are making the room in which our children sleep. The darker the room, the better the sleep. This aligns with the circadian rhythm, in that light signals our bodies to wake and dark signals it's time to slumber.

Young children may need some sort of night-light to sleep in their rooms, and I am absolutely not going to vilify that. However, try to reduce the brightness over time, and certainly try to use red or orange lights on the warm spectrum whenever possible. Experiment with different night-lights and sound machines if needed, to find the least possible light that helps your child feel comfortable and safe. Motion-sensing night-lights to lead the way to the bathroom are best, but again, meet your child where they are, as establishing confidence and a sense of safety at night is paramount to supporting strong sleep habits. This zone is meaningless if your little one is racked with nerves all night while lying in their über-dark bed with an empty stomach.

THEY LIKE TO MOVE IT, MOVE IT

We cannot talk about sleep without talking about movement. I admit that I thought stillness and quiet bodies set us up best for dreamland. But then I had children. More specifically, I had *my* children.

My idea of an optimal bedtime routine consisted of a warm, Epsom salt bath, lullaby music, books, snuggles, prayers, and pass out. My husband, however, seemed to inspire a different vibe at bedtime. We had plenty of nights as he traveled for work to experiment with different nighttime routines. Mine was usually the aforementioned chill.

His, however, resembled something out of WWE. There was jumping, throwing, screeching, and usually someone took it too far at some point and ended up in tears... before insisting, "Do it again!" In other words, it's pre-bed calamity. My bossy, Type-A self balked at this display of chaos mere minutes before bedtime was meant to start, sure that this would result in wired children, ready to wrestle instead of read.

To be fair, this is sometimes absolutely the case, especially when immediately preceding pillow time. However, many nights, I noticed that this rowdy ritual seemed to help expel whatever wiggles were still brewing within their little bodies.

I later learned about proprioceptive input and its role in sleep preparation for some children, and realized that there was actually a scientific reason for why these rambunctious romps leading up to bedtime actually helped my kiddos calm.

For some sensory-seeking children (like my son and daughter), getting in some physical feedback in the form of jumping, rolling, pushing, and pulling helps their vestibular system get exactly what it needs to calm. This can also help prepare a child to sit still during mealtimes or in the classroom (which is yet another reason why the decline in recess at schools is a travesty).

Optimally, this happens at least 15 minutes before bedtime. But especially if you have a busy, active little one, try to incorporate this type of physical "work" into your pre-bed routine to help this zone take root.

RELEASE THE PRESSURE

It's surprising that I've only mentioned Kim John Payne's book *Simplicity Parenting* once thus far, but in chatting about releasing those pre-bed wiggles with some physical work, it's also important to understand Payne's concept of "pressure valves." These are moments created throughout the day that provide kids with an opportunity to let off steam, be it physically, emotionally, or mentally. Regular "puffs" of steam release prevent a massive build up, curtailing bedtime explosions.

Every child is different, and letting off steam will mean different things and take place via different means. But consider for a moment your own life: Have you ever taken some breaks throughout a busy work day to take a walk, call a friend, grab a yoga class, or punch your way through kickboxing? These are adult versions of pressure valves, and the value-add to your overall regulation and cognition throughout the day translates for kids as well.

Recess is a beautiful example of a well-established (albeit waning) pressure valve for most children who attend school. Rest or nap time in preschool is another important pressure valve. For some children, the after school-tradition of cuddling on the couch and watching a favorite show is a much-needed respite from rambunctious classmates and cognitive demands. Quiet time with a book, working a puzzle, free play on the play set in the backyard, calisthenics and stretching, a sweaty game of tag with their sibling, or even a really good cry are all examples of ways that children can release the pressure that builds up throughout the day. This has everything to do with sleep, too. As Payne says, "A pressure valve lets a child release emotional steam. When they can let it go during the day, they can more easily 'let go' into sleep."

Cultivating and encouraging moments throughout your children's days, observing when they need some extra or a specific type of release, is one of the most powerful ways you can help them come into bedtime a little less hot.

GET IN THE ZONE

- Throw out the rule book and find what works for your family
- Proactively prioritize sleep for your kids—don't wait for signs
- Shoot for consistent bedtimes and wake times
- Eat at least two hours before bed
- Avoid caffeine for young children, and no later than noon for teens
- Get early morning sunlight on your eyes, and theirs, as soon as possible after waking
- Reduce blue and overhead bright lights in the evening
- Try blue-light-blocking glasses and amber lighting for evening activities
- Avoid devices and screens several hours before bed
- Prioritize movement before bedtime (at least fifteen minutes prior) to release the wiggles
- Help your child create pressure valves throughout the day for better regulation at bedtime

CROSSING GUARDS

- Andy Crouch — *The Tech-Wise Family: Everyday Steps for Putting Technology in Its Proper Place*
- Kim John Payne, MED and Lisa M. Ross — *Simplicity Parenting: Using the Extraordinary Power of Less to Raise Calmer, Happier, and More Secure Kids*
- Taylor Kulik Sleep and Wellness — *https://taylorkulik.com/*
- Tech Wellness blue light blockers — *https://techwellness.com/collections/blue-light*
- The Lullaby Trust — *https://www.lullabytrust.org.uk/*
- William Stixrud, PhD and Ned Johnson — *The Self-Driven Child: The Science and Sense of Giving Your Kids More Control Over Their Lives*

Chapter 4

MINDFUL MEDIA

If I could pick one chapter of this book to share beyond the scope of parents and caregivers, it would be this one. While there are many examples of the ways in which our modern, American culture isn't kid-friendly, media is particularly offensive on this front because it's *everywhere*.

Just the other day while driving in traffic, I saw a bumper sticker with a saying that included profanity in large, block letters, and thought, *Man, I'm glad my four-year-old can't read yet.* There are ads for fruity alcoholic drinks enticing anyone within earshot to "Have a great time!" at the gas pump where I refuel my (super-cool) minivan. Every time I turn on our family TV to pull up a show for my kids' downtime (see, I don't hate the television), I have to scroll like a banshee to avoid the movie thumbnails of demonic clowns and creepy villains in the major streaming apps. (Take a hint,

Netflix and Hulu. These viewers never have nor will need *Hateful Hobgoblins IV* front and center at selection time.)

What's tricky when we talk about media is that we don't need to consider only the content, an obvious focal point of this section, but also the sheer volume of media to which children are exposed every day, everywhere. Waiting rooms, classrooms, bathrooms, dash-mounted in vehicles, on wrists, and in every pocket and purse in America, screens abound.

I am not suggesting we all turn into Luddites, but just as we discussed with food in Chapter 2, media is also not neutral. We have allowed devices and connectivity to become so ubiquitous that the reach of media has gone unchecked, and we tend to normalize its presence without any evaluation of safety or even prudence. But for this zone, we're going to do exactly that.

We have a preponderance of evidence that pervasive media—shows, movies, music, apps, emails, ads, pop-ups, widgets, you name it—is not a good thing. Sure, it is easier than ever to get information at your fingertips, but most people aren't walking encyclopedias as a result. Grammar is degrading year over year, and many folks couldn't form a cohesive argument, free of logical fallacies, if their lives depended on it.

Granted, it's no sweat to stay in touch, yet people of all ages are feeling lonelier and more disconnected than ever despite 24/7 connectivity. You don't have to miss a single moment of someone else's life; meanwhile, we're not present for our real, authentic life. We have access to every perspective imaginable, and it seems we're growing more intolerant and uprooted generation by generation.

The barrage of media and the accessibility of hyper-connected devices constitute a giant experiment into which we've opted as a culture... minus the informed consent. I don't recall a time in which we collectively stopped to consider the implications of such change, and we can scarcely catch our breath before another new technology is introduced that doubles down on the normalcy of connectivity and information overload that already marks our modern consciousness.

We're moving far too quickly to respond to the emerging studies and data points that indicate that media proliferation is problematic and needs some recalibration. Anyone advocating for pumping the brakes is labeled anti-technology and basically laughed out of the public sphere (or rather, the bastardized version of what's left of it).

Folks, I am asking *you* to slow down.

What I cannot do is give you specific dos and don'ts for your family. I may hold a different worldview than you do, I have different children than you do, and we may have different necessities in terms of media than you do. I will, however, lean on the experts and valuable voices in this area to share some insights worth considering when deciding what kind of media and devices are welcome in your home.

I'm not going to lie; this zone may warrant the biggest jackhammer. It requires that you rethink your own usage of devices and what media you're consuming, as well as that of your children. If you've already given your kid a smartphone or a tablet, that doesn't mean it's too late. Pulling back on technology is one of the more difficult things to ask of someone, which in and of itself speaks volumes. But as we'll see, it may be the most important intervention you make.

Let's examine some of the data and trends that we have accessible at our fingertips... as does every policy-maker, organization leader, and caregiver today. But we're actually going to respond to it. Like, *now.* Let's do our due diligence in considering the impact of media on children—*our* children—and heed the advice of those who are willing to be laughed off the stage, shadow banned, or canceled to get the word out that all is not quiet on the Western front. One household at a time, we're going to engage in mindful media.

IT WAS A SIMPLER TIME

It is not hyperbole to say that I am older than Google. I was born pre-Wi-Fi. I didn't have an email address until my late teens, no online accounts of any sort until I enrolled in college, and no cell phone until I was in my early twenties. (I did have a pager in high school, and to be honest, I'm still not sure what value that device provides.) I lived across the country from my parents in college and traveled Europe for a month with a calling card in tow. (For you young folks, calling cards were prepaid minutes tied to what looked like a credit card that required no fewer than seventy-five buttons pressed to make a call.) Most of my early memories were captured on a video camera the size of an infant or a point-and-click camera that required a trip to the drug store to fetch hard copies of our photos, only about 10 percent of which were non-blurry, and 80 percent guaranteed red eyes.

As a child growing up in the '80s and '90s, I was one of the last generations blessed with the gift of growing up without the constant barrage of media we know today. To go through puberty without social media was a sweet mercy. To exist fully in the moment, boredom and all, was an imperative we didn't know we needed in childhood. Relying on a trip to the library for school assignments and forcing our brains to remember song lyrics at will cultivated a love-hate relationship with work and accomplishment.

There were encyclopedias and microfiche. TV wasn't a babysitter, and no one batted an eyelash when our parents shut off the tube and told us to go outside and play. Those were literally the only instructions, and they were enough. We knew the assignment.

This is not childhood today. We've exchanged challenge and free space for ease and preoccupation. It is a bad trade. While a life of ease may sound pretty sweet, it's actually antithetical to what we need to thrive. Specifically, it's counterproductive to what children need to develop and flourish. Child-development experts point to necessities such as free, unstructured play (more on this in Chapter 5), physical challenges with an acceptable measure of danger, and in-person social engagement to properly and optimally wire an emerging child's brain and body for adolescence and adulthood.

Unchecked media and an abundance of devices directly threaten all of these vital aspects of development, effectively accomplishing what social psychologist Jonathan Haidt calls "rewiring" young brains in ways that have troubling outcomes. These concerns aren't hypothetical nor hyperbole. It's not difficult to see how much preteens and teenagers have changed over the years, but to observe the national trends demonstrating just how unwell adolescents (in particular) are is troubling.

With the advent of the smartphone, particularly Apple's iPhone in 2007, we began our collective shift toward constant connectivity. A few nights ago, I was watching the movie *The Holiday* with my husband, and I remarked how unusual it was to see the protagonist sitting on a train looking out the window. No phone in hand, no presumed scrolling her socials. (The movie was made in 2006.) How jarring that the sight of someone simply sitting, untethered to a screen or device, seems so foreign.

More and more teens graduated from flip phones to smartphones as the technology became a commodity. Social media had been around for a few years, but as smartphone-only apps such as Instagram and Snapchat emerged, the pull toward those tiny computers in our pockets and purses became much more powerful.

And young brains are most vulnerable to this pull. If you can imagine someone charged with developing the most enticing, addictive means to get users to engage with something, then the introduction and influence of social media apps make complete sense. The immediate feedback and gratification are more effective than endlessly pulling on a slot machine's handle waiting for a hit, because the dopamine "hits" are constant. (We'll discuss dopamine more soon.)

Not only are kids feeding into their insatiable desires for *more! new! now!* with social media like TikTok and Snapchat, but the influence of these apps has an incredibly efficient social learning impact. Please don't hear "learning" and think that's a good thing. What children are learning via social media is sadly how to be more like other children on social media. Kids are teaching kids, and the outcomes are abysmal.

One of the most insightful and powerful commentaries on media and children is Jonathan Haidt's *The Anxious Generation: How the Great Rewiring of Childhood Is Causing an Epidemic of Mental Illness.* If you can find the time, I highly recommend this book to everyone, parent or not. (Dr. Haidt is a frequent podcast guest, so you could also search for some of his interviews. Regardless, you won't want to miss his rally cry for parents, administrators, and legislators on this subject.)

The book highlights of particular concern how social media "teaches" young users via an incredibly effective yet shallow means. As Haidt describes, "In a real-life social setting, it takes a while—often weeks—to get a good sense for what the most common behaviors are.... But on a social media platform, a child can scroll through a thousand data points in one hour (at three seconds per post), each one accompanied by numerical evidence (likes) and comments to show whether the post was a success or failure. *Social media platforms are therefore the most efficient conformity engines ever invented* (emphasis mine)."

Conformity engines. What a staggering and yet appropriate term for these apps, which seem to grow and morph year over year. (I don't even know what half of them are, to be honest.) We cannot idly stand by and watch our kids conform to a new normal for pre-teens and teenagers that is marred by anxiety and depression. The sullen teenager archetype cannot be a self-fulfilling prophecy in which we simply expect years of tumult and unhappy children and therefore assuage the common behaviors associated with heavy device and social media usage.

The data has shown significant spikes in mental health problems, including ER visits, that cannot be accounted for by economic shifts or genetic changes. Much of this shift happened exactly as the prevalence of smartphones (especially among teenagers) increased, between 2010 and 2015. And the rates of depression and anxiety are still climbing. We haven't leveled off, folks.

Young brains simply cannot engage with social media well. Their brains are actively forming throughout childhood, and exposure to these apps quite literally changes how their brains develop. This isn't about technological literacy, which can be accomplished with limited, prudent access to devices with developmentally appropriate apps. Social media is a free-for-all.

There are specific ages, too, for which the exposure to social media apps is worse than others. According to Haidt, ages 11 to 13 are considered the worst for girls, while boys are most impacted at ages 14 to 15. But don't assume you're in the clear if your children are outside of this age range. Sapien Labs has conducted a study as part of the *Global Mind Project*, examining global well-being across several metrics, and they concluded in October 2024 that the later the age at which young adults acquire a smartphone or tablet—not social media access, but internet-connected devices—the better their well-being scores into adulthood.

And the converse is true: "Those who got their first phone at a younger age were more likely to experience suicidal thoughts, feelings of aggression toward others and a sense of being detached from reality." The negative trends associated with early phone ownership were more severe for young girls. We have to take seriously the inquiries into social media companies, such as the hearing before the US Congress in January 2024, after which South Carolina Senator Lindsey Graham said, "After years of working on this issue... I've come to conclude the following: Social media companies as they're currently designed and operate are dangerous products."

As of November 2024, Australia has announced proposed legislation that would ban social media accounts to anyone under sixteen years of age. Australian Prime Minister Anthony Albanese was quoted in *The New York Times* as saying, "Social media is doing harm to our kids and I'm calling time on it. I've spoken to thousands of parents, grandparents, aunties and uncles. They, like me, are worried sick about the safety of our kids online."

We are the parents and caregivers. We cannot and should not wait for governing bodies or the companies who produce (and profit from) these products to act. The data is not nuanced or unclear. Social media and constant media access are hurting our children and precluding optimal development. And we simply cannot allow that to happen to the ones we love.

MIND-NUMBING

Just a few decades ago, the idea of sitting on the couch, scrolling through social media on a smartphone with a TV blaring in the background, surrounded by family members doing the same, would have sounded like some sort of dystopian social experiment. Yet not only has it been normalized, but it's actually socially accepted as an effective form of relaxation and quality time. (Spoiler alert: It's neither.) Urban Dictionary has even added the term "alone together" to its online dictionary, a phrase coined by Sociologist and MIT professor Sherry Turkle in her 2011 book of the same title. But her work wasn't put forth to assign a name to a new means of social hangs; it was meant to be a warning.

Doomscrolling on a smartphone without a clear purpose or objective is not only a killer of meaningful productivity and human-to-human interaction, but it's also not great for your mental health. The constant barrage of content and information, not to mention notifications and feedback—likes, hearts, comments, and follows—is a giant dopamine frenzy for your brain. Dopamine has a necessary function in our brains for survival, encouraging affinity for the kinds of things that help keep us alive and sustained.

I hope I don't have to explain how spending hours on the couch, in the car, or in bed staring at a bright screen are hardly necessary for survival. Instead, that natural reward system has been overloaded by the hits we get when plugged into our phones, and our baseline for the number of stimuli needed to elicit pleasure is actually *increased*. In other words, the more we engage, the less we can satisfy. (Dr. Anna Lembke's *Dopamine Nation: Finding Balance in the Age of Indulgence* is an excellent study in understanding how dopamine addiction works, the painful implications of dopamine overload, and how to counterbalance those impacts to reset healthy homeostasis.)

We struggle with this as adults with fully formed prefrontal cortexes. Meaning, we are fully equipped to make wise choices and abstain from things that hinder us, and yet mindless scrolling is still a norm for many of us. Imagine being a child with under-developed skills in making optimal long-term choices and ill-equipped at coping with addictive behaviors.

It's not a pretty picture, especially when young brains are actively firing and wiring at all times. Introducing addictive technology and over-stimulating media literally sets the baseline for the brain at levels that cannot be sustained. These maladaptations impact learning and cognition, manifest as behavioral issues, and can even hinder the ability for children to foster long-term relationships.

When the brain is wired for *more! new! now!* we establish a frenetic pace that calibrates the brain to seek more hits at every chance, shunning anything that interferes with getting said hits, be it jobs, meals, or even relationships.

To say that internet-connected devices act like drugs in the brain is not an overstatement. Constant connectivity works in a similar mechanism as getting high in terms of how it impacts the brain, albeit on a reduced scale. But when you consider that spending hours in front of a screen isn't socially scorned like shooting up in public, we've normalized an all-day IV drip of the drug-of-choice.

Sadly, no one bats an eyelash—in part, because we're all riveted to our screens, too. When Silicon Valley innovators and social media app creators don't allow their own children to use many of the devices and apps normalized for our kids—at ever-younger ages—we have to take pause and consider what they know that we don't.

I realize I've painted a bleak picture, but this isn't a hypothetical warning. We've had those for decades now and no one seemed to heed them. (Remember, *1984* was written in 1948.) I don't think I have to convince anyone that this is where we are. But I refuse to believe that we should just lie down, grab our phones, and let it be. Heck, no! As the adults, we are more than capable of taking back our households, taking back our kids, and, eventually, taking back our communities.

We can wire up a zone that encourages real-life, actual communication, and true connection. We can wean our kids (and each other) off the cheap highs of blue-screen-driven dopamine hits. And we can choose to spend our time differently, fruitfully, to have something to show for our days.

YOU CAN'T UNTOAST THE TOAST

One of the most profound things I've ever heard came from the mouth of a then-seven-year-old. It was at one of the Wednesday gatherings with the group of mothers with whom I was doing life circa 2018, and our children of varying ages were playing together in a nearby living room while we laughed, cried, and prayed together.

It was not uncommon for the TV to be on in the background for the kids, though most of them ignored whatever episode of *Paw Patrol* was on repeat, instead diving into the mounds of novel toys or running around in the spacious backyard. (Yes, there was a tire swing. It was as idyllic as it sounds.)

Courtney, a mother sage beyond her years, was sharing with us that her son had recently had his first foray into media that made him uncomfortable. He didn't sneak a forbidden peek or anything of the sort, but instead wanted to watch a popular show he heard about from some of his peers, and so he made his case to Mom.

After a thoughtful discussion with his patient mother—warning of the intense content for his unique proclivities—she agreed to let him make the choice, and he proceeded to watch an episode of the show. Unfortunately, it didn't sit well for the boy, and he found himself ruminating on certain images from the episode, as well as feeling a general sense of unrest due to some of the hand-to-hand violence depicted.

What was beautiful about this example is that Courtney received him with a compassionate heart, understanding the tension between independence and prudence. There was no "I told you so." The lesson was self-evident for the young boy.

He said, "Mom, I get it now. You can't untoast the toast." He couldn't unsee what he had seen or unhear what he'd heard. And that is incredibly true for everyone who consumes media. Even if something is on in the background, children are absorbing everything in their environment, and even a glimpse may be enough to disturb young children.

I share this example because it's fairly easy to address media when children are really young. The less they have it or know about it, the easier it is to limit and control the content. If they've never heard of *Baby Shark* or *Paw Patrol*, you won't get the accompanying pleading meltdowns (or insidious songs stuck in your head). When there's no precedence of watching something on your iPhone, they won't ask for it.

But as children get older, they are inherently steeped in a media-consumed culture. Elementary children are aware of comic book villains even if those characters get no air time in your home. (My six-year-old was shown a terrifying picture of Venom by a classmate and it rocked his world for days... or nights, to be precise.) Even without a device of their own, kids still know the names of popular social media apps.

We have to take the proactive approach. That's the name of the game when it comes to the mindful media zone. It is wise to talk to children early and often about media, and not only about what they can and can't watch. Help them understand your goals when it comes to media, what role media can and should play in their own lives, and how to discern what safe media looks like... as well as how to deal with exposures or invitations to unsafe media. (*Good Pictures Bad Pictures* by Kristen A. Jenson may be a helpful resource for this conversation. There's a *Junior* version for younger kids, too.)

Do not assume your kids are too young to have these conversations. The earlier you communicate about how and why you chose the content and timing of the media you encourage in your home, the more coaching your children will have, and the more opportunity for repetition to aid in retention. Keep the door open for conversations along the way, knowing this is a zone that will be important for many years, and do your best not to react to the content of their questions or concerns. Play it cool and they'll know you can take the really hard conversations when they come, too.

WHOA, THAT WAS INTENSE...

Something that we don't talk enough about when it comes to children is intensity. While intensity in and of itself isn't a bad thing, when it comes to media that is intense, we need to be very careful about how and when we expose kids to such things. If you've spent any time around children, you already know that we could be saying something as innocuous as the alphabet, but if we're saying it with a stern tone, we're going to get a reaction from young ones.

How information is conveyed or presented matters, and certainly the power or seriousness with which some media presents to still-developing minds and bodies can have a significant impact on the felt experience of consuming that media.

When children and adults alike go through the emotions of stress, our bodies feel it. Said another way, imagined stress is experienced as actual stress. Our genes served us for thousands of years by preparing us to run from lions and bears, but most of us are still running from imaginary lions and bears on a daily basis.

Our bodies aren't meant for that, and our spirits certainly aren't either. Feigned fear or excitement, such as that experienced with high-intensity films, shows, music, etc., is very much interpreted by our bodies as real. It will deplete. It costs something. And for children, that price is much too high.

Films and television shows provide ratings to help parents gauge age-appropriateness, but it's worth knowing that intensity isn't explicitly assessed except for intense violence (garnering an R rating). Unfortunately, a rated-R movie doesn't mean that children can't see it; it simply means that children under seventeen years old must be accompanied by a parent or adult guardian, enforcement of which is voluntary. (You can view the Rating Classifications yourself at *filmratings.com/RatingsGuide*, which I recommend for all parents at least once to get an understanding of what is and isn't considered in their rating rules.)

Common Sense Media is a helpful resource for assessing age-appropriateness for various media—including games, apps, and websites—and while it doesn't specifically include an intensity rating, their rating system does take into account social and emotional development factors.

Without a well-defined system for judging intensity, how is a parent to proceed? Here are a few things to keep an eye out for that may signal age-inappropriate intensity:

- Depictions of overly-romantic relationships between teenagers
- Frequent scene changes and flashing lights (particularly for younger viewers)
- Dark themes, such as demons, magic, zombies, monsters
- Gory imagery, such as bloodshed, dismemberment, blood splatter (even if non-human)
- Loud and powerful music, especially coupled with vivid imagery
- Depictions of extreme anguish or peril, especially for the protagonist

Keep in mind, too, that cartoons and graphic novels marketed for children are not absolved when it comes to watching for excessive intensity. Consider, for example, the growing concerns from parents and advocacy groups about anime and manga, in part due to the intense imagery and themes. Just because something looks kid-friendly in medium or format does not mean that the content isn't worth examining... ideally *before* your child partakes.

TUNE IN TO YOUR KID

The most important thing you can do as a parent and caregiver when it comes to media is this: *Watch your child.* You may have heard great things about a show or site, checked ratings and pre-screened for approval, but don't forget to pay attention to your specific kid.

Do they appear tense, nervous, irritable, or concerned while watching or listening? Are they ignoring other stimuli in their physical space, such as sound or people in the room? Can they easily walk away from the media or do they seem sucked in? What one kid can watch or hear without consequence, another may not. And that's frankly all the data you need. If nightmares and difficult behaviors follow, then reduction or elimination is the right call.

(Note: If you suspect your child is having an unusual reaction to media, it is perfectly OK to seek guidance from your healthcare provider or a licensed counselor. We don't need to judge it, and it's not a commentary on you as a parent. Ruling out sensory concerns or underlying emotional issues can go a long way if you feel like your child is showing a pattern of struggling with certain types of media exposures.)

Remember: You are the parent. In the words of parenting coach Jill Savage, "Technology may be here to stay, but so are parents; both play a major role in our [children's] lives." If an upcoming slumber party includes movie night, make sure you've asked what movie they will be watching, and set expectations with your kid about how they should handle it if another movie is chosen, such as a scary film.

When my son's school allows the occasional film on Friday afternoons, I have communicated proactively to the his teacher that I would like to know the movie title in advance. If it's a movie I am not comfortable with him viewing, he stays home. It's that simple. Everyone in our children's lives—grandparents, aunts/uncles, friends, babysitters—understand our mindful media guidelines, and we communicate them proactively and reiterate them often. If that understanding is breached (such as by allowing unsupervised time on YouTube), we discuss our guidelines and our "why" again. With repeated offense, we limit or discontinue unsupervised time with that caregiver.

My children also understand not only how we observe these guidelines—the specific dos and don'ts—but also why they exist. I don't require that my children approve our approach, but I am playing the long game and use every opportunity I can to help them understand how we protect them now, so they can protect themselves and make strong choices in the future.

Dr. Kathy Koch, author of *Screens and Teens: Connecting with Our Kids in a Wireless World*, encourages this approach, explaining, "Influencing our teens regarding technology is going to hinge on a lot of communication—discussions about their choices and ours, sharing reasons for the choice we make, listening to one another with affection and respect."

With proactive communication (and a lot of it), children and adolescents have agency in choosing how they observe our family norms for media consumption, and the grown-ups in their lives are there to provide bumpers when they've stumbled into unknown territory or are simply testing boundaries, as children of all ages are wont to do.

You may be reading this section and thinking what a buzzkill I must be as a mom... or worse. I take no offense to it. I am the one who has to answer for how I steward my children, who my husband and I know better than anyone else. When many modern children are technology-obsessed, distracted, anxious, and irritable, we are more than OK with being odd. Not to mention, we feel these very real effects of media in our own lives. Even as I write this, I'm having to consciously *not* pick up my phone to see what's going down on Instagram or pop on an episode of *Friends*.

The struggle is real, and it's actually great to share this in our conversations with our kiddos. We can model where we have to abstain for the sake of productivity or wellness, and seeing us walk the walk is incredibly impactful, especially for adolescents.

Imagine what a different culture we could cultivate if we provided the kind of homes and communities where kid-friendly, developing-brain-appropriate, consciously curated media was the norm. Where we don't have to police environments for what needs to be weeded out to protect little minds and bodies, expecting the current deluge of crap.

Where doctor's offices appeal to the youngest possible patient in terms of which movies they show on their waiting room TVs. (My one-year-old was pretty shaken up while waiting on a croup diagnosis at the sight of a fiery Te Kā fiercely clawing after Moana. Thanks a heap, Urgent Care for Kids.) Or better yet, where every single moment isn't infused with noise and screens, a topic we'll dive into more next.

This zone pays dividends when it expands well beyond our homes. Churches, schools, community centers, restaurants, and event centers are the very fabric of gathering places for our communities. We cannot continue to fill these spaces with screens and provide entertainment at every angle our necks can possibly turn. We should not slight our youngest, most vulnerable, and most impressionable members of society.

They are always watching. We're constantly bombarded by hyper-sexualized imagery, innuendo, or straight-up profanity. (Hey, trampoline park, maybe rap music about getting drunk in da club isn't the optimal choice for a Saturday morning bounce session.) What does it say about our society that we insist, "Avert your eyes, children. The grown-ups gotta have it." This status quo approach to public media is really troubling. It's time to put the children first!

SWEET STILLNESS

Not nearly present enough in the conversation when it comes to media is how vital it is for children to be able to function in silence. Many neurotypical children find it difficult to function these days without a screen in front of their face or an AirPod in their ear. (I specify neurotypical children because neurodivergent children have differing needs and baseline abilities. For the sake of this discussion, we're talking about children who do not have any diagnosed condition that inhibits their inherent ability to be still and quiet.) Abstaining from stimuli is an important aspect of this zone to ensure that we don't forsake the importance of tolerating quiet, even if the media from which we are abstaining is considered safe.

Dr. Amy Sullivan, a clinical health psychologist at the Cleveland Clinic was interviewed on the topic of stillness in 2020, and said, "Learning to sit in stillness and self-reflect is one of the greatest gifts we can give ourselves and our kids. When we look internally and delve deeper into our value system and wants and needs, we can communicate at a deeper level. We have to foster that ability."

The fostering aspect of this ability is especially poignant as parents. This doesn't just happen, certainly not in our current hustle and bustle culture, glued to screens on the regular. Yes, we need sensory breaks, but this is also about being comfortable with ourselves, something that increasingly feels like a dying art. The ability to be still and introspect is one that must be taught and nurtured, and we own this responsibility when it comes to young people.

Not only should we create space in our households and classrooms for quiet time—literally, time without sound, not just quiet for Mama or Teacher—but we should help our children cultivate their own sense of value for this practice, as the benefits last into adulthood. We could all use more of this.

Similar to the benefits of gathering at the table for family mealtime, creating media-free rhythms throughout your family's days can help open windows for connection, restoration, and coaching. (Sounds like a pressure valve, doesn't it?) I often learn most about my children on the commute to school or as we're lying down for bedtime. Had we infused music or screens into these times, I may very well have missed out on an opportunity to connect with my favorite people.

And listen, I'm not saying that you can't listen to some tunes on the drive to school. We have different expectations for car time if we're going on a road trip, for example, than we do for the thirty-minute drive to school. And we do occasionally watch a show or movie while we eat dinner, as you'll recall. But it's not the norm.

The point is to ensure that your child has regular, expected times throughout their days when there is no media present. Look at where you are today, and consider where you can reduce device usage or noise, such as bath time, mealtimes, car rides, bedtime, before school, quiet time. In any of these rituals, media should never overtake the presence of family. Soft or low music in the background is very different from loud songs that compete with any chance of conversation.

When I hear my daughter say, "Mom, you're interrupting, I can't hear the music," while catching up with my son at pick-up, I know it's time to give the music a break. And because we've talked about it and set our expectations around this zone, my daughter may not love me shutting off her jam, but she certainly isn't surprised by it.

REVIVING SOCIAL ENGAGEMENT

We've alluded to the importance of abstinence from media for the sake of getting comfortable with ourselves and creating space for family conversations to flow. But it is worth a distinctive conversation to examine the ways in which children are morphing the ways they connect with their peers and other humans due to technology. It's probably not spoiling anything to tell you now that the trends are not good, but we need to look further to understand exactly what is at stake and why this is such an important area in which to intervene.

The practice of connecting live, in real life, with people plays an important role in our physical and emotional regulation. In general, school-aged children spend the majority of their waking hours during the week with their peers while attending school. They may not interact all that much in structured classrooms, but they're surrounded by other children their age for most of the day.

Inherently, peers are not as emotionally and mentally mature as adults, which means that kids need other resources to effectively manage their thoughts and feelings. School-aged children get the help they need by co-regulating, which simply means that parents, caregivers, or teachers will help a child who is struggling to manage their feelings, check their behaviors, and get back to a state of calm where they are no longer in fight-or-flight mode. In other words, until kids can self-regulate, they have to borrow our "chill" to react to stress in healthy, appropriate ways. (If you're thinking that you know some adults who still can't do this, you're not alone.)

Regulation and dysregulation—chill vs. no-chill—are important concepts to understand for this conversation because we want to ever-increasingly encourage our children in their abilities to self-regulate. Dysregulation is inevitable: the favorite pants aren't clean, they didn't make the team, their friend said or did something stupid, the blueberries are too blue... you get the picture.

What's key for future flourishing is for our children to learn regulating skills to cope with hardships (even if we think they're minuscule) and to exhibit self-control. If you've never heard about psychologist Walter Mischel's Marshmallow Test, go Google it now. Science proves that self-control and patience in youth predict positive outcomes over time. (And yes, I get the irony of asking you to pick up your phone during this chapter.)

Peers are stupid. Let's just say it. Children are fickle, arbitrary in one moment, black-and-white the next, and prone to resemble *Lord of The Flies* if left unchecked. (My son attends a learner-lead private school. Trust me, kids go savage fast.) But if we are resolved to accept that our kids spend much of their day among peers—true for many, not all, of course—we need to be incredibly aware of what the interactions with friends look like.

Not only do we want to coach against gossiping and bullying, obvious parenting fodder, but we also need to understand how these relationships are either assisting or conflicting with our kid's ability to regulate. Is this friendship stressful and chaotic, or is it reciprocal and healthy? Are they watching each other's faces and body language, or are they sitting next to each other with their noses glued to their smartphones?

Here's why this matters: If our children are spending their in-person time with friends well, then they are likely exercising their social engagement system (or "SES"), and experiencing the benefits of regulation through relationship. SES is an aspect of Dr. Stephen Porges's Polyvagal Theory, which posits that we have several means of constantly scanning and evaluating our environment for danger or for safety, and that these methods are largely unaware to us.

I promise I won't get too nerdy on you, but this theory is gaining traction in modern health and wellness circles as critical for managing the mental aspect of our holistic health, and it highlights the powerful connection between the mental and the physical.

As one of the stealth systems involved in how our nervous system is reacting to our current circumstances, the SES is an incredibly powerful method for establishing a sense of safety and telling our otherwise fight-or-flight-ready brains that we can chill out. (Similar mechanisms are important for *attunement* and *attachment*, terms you may have encountered in your parenting journey.) The importance of quality, person-to-person interactions, especially for child development, cannot be overlooked.

The reason I'm sharing all of this in the context of our discussion about media is that it's vital to understand that the SES is not activated the same way virtually as it is in person. Asynchronous, virtual, low buy-in connections do not assure our collectively over-tapped nervous systems, constantly spurred into dysregulation due to the continual barrage of activity and information.

Synchronous, face-to-face, high investment interactions, on the other hand, are actually therapeutic for the mind and the body. This is incredible! But the massive problem lies in the fact that, though we are increasingly tethered to one another, we are sacrificing regular SES activation and co-regulation via in-person communication and moving full speed toward the kind of connections that not only lack healing power, but they actually harm. We're trading secure attachments for anxious ones.

When smartphones became the norm for teenagers circa 2015, we didn't see relationships thriving and well-being indicators soar with the increased connectivity. Instead, we saw a rise in what Haidt calls "Internalizing Disorders," such as anxiety and depression, meaning the source of discontentment was from within. (The call is coming from inside the house.)

Girls transitioned their lives to social media apps, and boys tended to dive headfirst into video games or other virtual worlds, including pornography. While chats and comments were still part of their lives, the interactions hardly constituted real friendships, and the lack of genuine, meaningful social engagement created a troubling gap of feeling so alone in a culture in which you were never really disconnected.

Haidt remarks, "With so many new and exciting virtual activities, many adolescents (and adults) lost the ability to be fully present with the people around them, which changes social life for everyone, even for the small minority that did not use these platforms."

Genesis 2:18 says, "It is not good for the man to be alone." We were not designed to function solo, or to subsist on shallow, virtual relationships. I believe that the longing that our young people are feeling but don't know how to express is evidence of this. Young children are glued to devices, just waiting for *something* to which they can react, but nothing really matters. When a like from a random stranger garners the same reaction or longing as a long text from an old friend, none of it is significant.

I'm sure you've experienced the resigned disappointment of gathering with people for a meal or attending an event, only for those around you to spend the majority of the time on their phones, potentially even messaging the people sitting next to them. We give kids a hard time about it, but how often are we guilty of the very same thing?

We are sacrificing social engagement, that which reminds us that we're safe and rooted, and instead clamoring toward transient communication that reinforces addiction and keeps our minds and bodies in states of stress and lack. We are refusing the antidote while stoking the problem. Anxiety expert Dr. Russell Kennedy explains, "The more safety you create in your body, the less you will need to distract and dissociate into compulsive, worrisome thinking." But the opposite is true as well.

According to Drs. Neufeld and Maté, "The best prevention for an obsessive preoccupation with digital intimacy is healthy relational development." Be the family and home that fights the good fight for social engagement by making your kids wait on getting a smartphone, by limiting time spent on devices when friends are present, and by cultivating opportunities for your kids to do some real, good ol' fashioned socialization. Help them co-regulate until they've mastered self-regulation. Bring back ice cream after school and long walks with the dog. Leave the phones at home and watch your kids embody the sense of safety that actually satisfies.

TECHNOLOGY IS NOT A RIGHT

Cue the groans. But you know it's true: Technology is not a right. Sure, it can be convenient and, in some cases, required.

But in all cases, devices and media should be carefully considered before unleashing them in our homes and allowing them for our children. Ubiquity doesn't equal necessity, so don't get sucked into what culture would tell us. Be the buffers that understand needs versus wants on behalf of our children.

I suspect we'd see a lot less drama when it comes to apps and devices if we didn't hand over smartphones until our children were old enough to pay for them. A Marketplace.org article reports that teen employment is finally on the rise as of 2023, bouncing back from the COVID-19 pandemic and preceding years of decline, with the number of teens in the market for a job or already working hitting the highest annual rates since 2009.

Whether teens secure part-time work outside the home or start a side hustle mowing lawns or babysitting, encouraging the responsibility required to balance work, school, and home can be a great precursor to the responsibilities required to own a device, pay for it, and steward it in terms of time management.

Beyond smartphones, it is worth re-thinking the implications of introducing video game consoles into homes, especially if you're considering allowing devices in bedrooms. Are you prepared for the disappearance of your child and the fights required to pry them away from the controller? Have you set expectations around how often and what kind of games will be appropriate? Do not simply slide a Switch or Xbox under the tree and expect things to play out well. Most kids cannot self-manage their time or attention, so let them borrow your skills.

Many classrooms provide children with access to laptops or tablets, or even good ol' computer labs. (High five if you remember the joy of sliding an Oregon Trail floppy disk into a bulky Macintosh.) We shouldn't assume that kids understand how to safely and wisely use the internet just because they have regular access at school. Make time to talk about appropriate uses of online time, in appropriate imagery or music, how to vet information and sources, and even how to properly position the computer to protect their little eyes and necks.

My son has a dedicated laptop that he's permitted by the school to bring home on evenings or weekends, but we've set the expectation that he won't spend any additional time on the computer once he's put in his hours at school. This is not only to encourage outside or free play with his sister (see Chapter 5), but also to reinforce my own healthy media habits as someone who works remotely and could easily get sucked into the laptop well into the evening. Don't set expectations for your children that you aren't willing to abide by (in an age-appropriate equivalent). More is caught than taught.

Privacy when it comes to devices for underage children is also not a right. Kids are not equipped to manage decisions like those available on the internet. I don't care what parental controls or apps are engaged, we cannot hand over devices and assume our kids are safe or know how to behave online. (I regularly see posts about new ways that predators or curious kiddos have worked around controls and blocks to engage in undesired activities.)

This isn't just about surveillance, but also about coaching, which is a really crucial job for a parent that is becoming less realized generation by generation. Just because young children look like digital natives, we still need to teach them simple things like how to utilize emojis.

Earlier this spring, my then-seven-year-old was allowed by his school to utilize Google Chat with his fellow learners for a brief period of time. They frequently dabble with tools like ChatGPT and Google productivity tools as a form of technological literacy, which I applaud. But teaching new tools often focuses on the how, not the what. Meaning, providing instruction on how to navigate the UI and get the tool to work as expected isn't the same as coaching on the content and how the tool is ultimately used.

My little dude mastered the intuitive user experience of chatting with friends, including launching and navigating video conference sessions. But when I noticed a string of fairly dramatic emojis one day while reviewing past messages—something I set the expectation that I would do periodically—I knew I had a teachable moment on my hands.

Simply setting the context that online chats should reflect conversations and feelings that we would express equally in person was a lightbulb moment for my kid, something we probably assumed was a given. But it clearly wasn't. Sending five red-faced angry emojis in a row in response to a ten-minute gap in chats from a friend didn't at all reflect his real feelings on the matter, and yet he was sending a message to the contrary that could have caused relational harm. Because we discussed it, his emoji use morphed into healthy, silly reflections of his true self, which is something we should all practice in whatever presence we have online.

Have the conversations, set the expectations, and create a sense of accountability when it comes to device usage and media consumption at any age. Empower your kids to successfully navigate this zone and stay vigilant for signs that they need more information or need help.

KID-FRIENDLY ALTERNATIVES

I've seen in many parenting forums that often moms and dads are unwilling to keep smartphones from children because of risks such as school shootings, sleepovers, inexperienced drivers, etc. I understand the desire to protect your kids. But we have to consider everything we've covered in this section and acknowledge that unfettered access to the internet, all the time, isn't safe. We overprotect them from perceived, statistically minute threats while failing to protect them from actual, well-demonstrated harm.

There are alternatives to handing an iPhone to a ten-year-old. To limit distractions while staying in touch or to establish an emergency touch point, consider throwing it back with a flip phone. If you're met with groans, share the fun fact that Academy Award-winner and acclaimed writer-director Christopher Nolan rocks a flip phone. The dude created the coolest Batman movie ever, so that's gotta have some street cred. (See *Crossing Guards* section for more alternatives.)

Technology can be an incredible thing. My primary job for the last dozen years has been in the technology field, so please don't read this and think I'm over here churning butter and cursing anything with a switch. I understand the tension between possibility and reality, between speed to market and prudence. In the United States, we tend to take an innocent-until-proven-guilty approach in many of these areas, whereas others adopt the precautionary principle, requiring evidence of safety before endorsing or allowing.

We can't control the satellites in the sky or the kind of movies getting made, but we sure as heck have a vital role in managing what sort of media and devices find a home in our homes. And more importantly, we have to play an ongoing part in educating our children about how to maintain this zone for themselves as they grow-up. We can't even imagine the kinds of tech our kids will have access to as adults, so focus on general principles that help them navigate the unknown with their well-being and humanity firmly at the forefront.

GET IN THE ZONE

- Encourage your community to engage in mindful media... this works best if we all participate
- Don't assume media and devices are safe because they're prevalent
- Eliminate (ideal) or at least limit social media for children—don't wait for the government to do it
- Take regular breaks from devices and connectivity (including news and social media) for healthy dopamine regulation
- Proactively communicate with children—early and often—about mindful media
- Keep an eye out for intensity when screening media for the family
- Above all else, watch your kid for signs that certain media needs management
- Communicate media boundaries with caregivers and keep them accountable
- Walk the walk: Take care in your own media usage and consumption
- Create pockets of stillness in your family rhythms
- Encourage real-life, face-to-face communication whenever possible
- Make teens earn their devices and keep them accountable
- Digital literacy includes teaching the what (content, value, vetting sources) as much as the how

CROSSING GUARDS

- Andy Crouch — *The Tech-Wise Family: Everyday Steps for Putting Technology in Its Proper Place*
- Anna Lembke, MD — *Dopamine Nation: Finding Balance in the Age of Indulgence*
- Common Sense Media — *https://www.commonsensemedia.org/*
- Daniel Siegel, MD and Tina Payne Bryson, PhD — *The Whole Brain Child: 12 Revolutionary Strategies to Nurture Your Child's Developing Mind*
- Gabb Phone or Watch — *gabb.com*
- Gordon Neufeld, PhD and Gabor Maté, MD — *Hold On to Your Kids: Why Parents Need to Matter More Than Peers*
- Jonathan Haidt, PhD — *The Anxious Generation: How the Great Rewiring of Childhood Is Causing an Epidemic of Mental Illness*
- Kathy Koch, PhD — *Screens and Teens: Connecting with Our Kids in a Wireless World*
- Kristen A. Jenson, MA — *Good Pictures Bad Pictures* and *Good Pictures Bad Pictures Jr.*
- Pinwheel Phone — *pinwheel.com*
- Sherry Turkle, PhD — *Alone Together: Why We Expect More from Technology and Less from Each Other*

Chapter 5

HONORING THE HOURS

There is something about the changing seasons that brings to light just how important are the rhythms throughout our days and in our homes. We get an up-close look at how changes in activity, sleep, and food can impact the way we meet the various stages of a day.

In the summer, bedtimes go out the window in favor of movie nights and swimming until we can't see in front of our faces. Come spring, we're trying to wind down our babies as the sun glares through the drapes, betraying our attempts at bedtime during Daylight Savings. Falling back in November infuses an additional hour in the day to play in the leaves as the sun sets or take a morning walk with the dog, no longer greeted upon waking with darkness. And winter welcomes us with cozy blankets, stealing unexpected naps to offset plenty of feasting and fanfare.

When children are very little, however, none of this really matters. You're always tired, day runs into night, and there is no real bedtime... just periods when you get longer naps than others. Teething, stuffy noses, and developmental "Leaps" remind us that we can technically survive on a few hours of sleep, but it ain't pretty. Any disruption in the norm elicits extra meltdowns and requires skilled negotiation to make it through a week.

But eventually—I promise, Mama/Daddy—you actually get to choose the schedules for your family, to create an intentional plan for how you spend your time as a family and apart, and to enjoy the fruits of your efforts.

Looking around at the way many families around us structure their days, I can't help but notice something: we busy. It seems there's a never-ending barrage of birthday parties, sporting events, field trips, extracurriculars (and their corresponding recitals/competitions/exhibitions), spirit days/nights/weeks, and more. Dinners are served on the go, arms reaching back from the driver's seat to distribute nuggets or pre-made sandwiches, Goldfish everywhere, and water bottles exceeding family members. Homework for one child happens while running around town for another child, and we keep totes in our trunks filled with changes of clothes, uniforms, school supplies, and extra snacks. None of this works without snacks.

It probably comes as no surprise that we don't keep this pace in the Gonzalez home. (Homie don't play that.) When my kids were still really young, I learned the importance of a light schedule, especially on weekends, for my own well-being while adjusting to motherhood with an anxious baseline and easily dysregulated nervous system. My "selfish" needs defined how we spent our days in those early years.

But as I spent many contact naps reading child development and health/wellness books (studying on the job), I learned that my needs aligned with those of my infant. He also needed a clear calendar to just unfold as a new human, take in his surroundings, and connect with his person: Mama.

As he grew, we of course ventured out into the world, but we still kept a prudent pace, spending hours at the park instead of jumping around play spaces and play dates. We'd take long walks to get Mama some coffee (we lived walking distance to a Starbucks for many years, bless it) or enjoy a leisurely stroll through the grocery store or local zoo.

Still, the majority of our day consisted of what I call "scientist mode." I'd let him spend hours exploring our home—inside and out—and our neighborhood, picking up every gadget, stick, and material he came across. The mouth usually got involved too, naturally. My role was obviously to keep him safe, but to also remain close as a quiet assurance that he could explore without fear, knowing I was still there.

I was like a scientific researcher, studying my subject in his natural habitat, and I spent hours a day observing him. This was honestly my greatest teacher as a new mom, and I continue to observe my children often. Still to this day, my four-year-old daughter will play for hours knowing my presence is nearby, but not involved with or directing her play. Even if she asks me to join, she takes the lead, and I follow. This is her territory, after all.

Following the status quo would require that the older my children get, the more we'd sign up for, and the less frequently we'd have an event-free weekend. Less time for them to simply *exist* in their natural habitat. But when most kids are exhausted, anxious, and unwell, we have to look at the common activities and schedules of modern children and acknowledge that they're too much. Our society/culture hasn't embraced a pace for childhood that is based on child development insights and research. The norm is largely based on and fueled by fear, be it of falling behind, of missing "enrichment," or of not looking impressive enough for college admissions.

Many of us have overlooked just how intense are the expectations of young children because we are steeped ourselves in hustle culture, ignoring our own role in grooming our children earlier and earlier to expect this pace into adulthood. An eighty-hour work week is no sweat if you've been running on the hamster wheel since age five.

Children are not mini-adults. Not even close. When we forget to honor what children need to thrive and develop optimally, we hinder their long-term abilities to be successful and balanced. The very thing we're trying to ensure, we actually threaten when we push hard and fast for outcomes. We're burning out our babies.

As Kim John Payne describes it, "As a society we've 'enriched' our kids' schedules, ironically, to the point of overuse and depletion. The overscheduled child is like soil that has been constantly and extensively cropped. Without rest and replenishment... it becomes compacted, a dust bowl."

I am confident that every parent, caregiver, teacher, and relative wants to see the children they love flourish, vibrant and deeply rooted. No one wishes for a barren dust bowl.

So how do we navigate this zone? How can we ensure our kids don't busy away their childhood and miss out on all they need to make it?

The answer is play.

THE WORK OF PLAY

Children who do not get adequate play are hardly children at all. It's infused in their very being to learn and grow via play. I'm not talking about adult-lead activities that involve laughter and some movement. Play at its core is spontaneous, child-led, fully immersive, physical, and unstructured. It's piles of sticks that become villagers or cities, obstacle courses built with toys and found objects, games with rules that morph and coalesce as the play unfolds, rowdy wrestling with a sibling, and dress-up that transforms and drives imaginative narratives forward.

Do you remember being a kid and spending hours with cardboard boxes, stuffies, and craft supplies, nary a parent in sight, checking in, or offering advice? I do, and it was spectacular. But this birthright of childhood is endangered, edged out by structured events, play dates, sports, and "enrichment."

As Dr. MacNamara, child-development expert and clinical counselor, asserts in her book *Rest, Play, Grow*, "There is no greater task in raising young children today than creating the conditions that will protect the space and time for play. It means pushing back against the cultural tide that sees play as frivolous and unproductive instead of as the bedrock upon which our children realize their full human potential." Dr. MacNamara is calling for us to establish a zone that cultivates play.

Play is intentionally within our chapter on schedules because what children really need to execute this zone *is* time. Adults actually own a very small role in shaping the form that play takes, as kids are the chiefs of free play. The less hands-on we are, the more they can test their limits and expand their ideas. We're vigilant when it comes to media (as discussed in Chapter 4), but we back off big time when it comes to play. Given the dwindling hours in many children's schedules for this kind of spontaneous activity, however, managing schedules is exactly where we come in here. Sure, providing open-ended toys and tools is a great way to fuel their play, but keep in mind that young people can make a game or adventure out of anything. The only raw material really required is children with time to spare.

TIME TRADE-OFFS

As the parents or guardians, we decide which events and activities make their way onto our calendars, stewarding our hours and funds as a family unit. To pave this zone, we need to get really comfortable and willing to say, "No." There are a gazillion things vying for our time and attention, and if you don't have your priorities in check, it's easy to let life kind of happen to you. (Roll over you, it feels like.)

Let someone else volunteer in the classroom. Let your kiddo go a whole semester without a sport or after-school activity. Let that random parent think you're lame for declining their child's birthday party invitation. And most importantly... let your kids be bored. Let them.

Filling our days with activities costs something. Literally, of course... this stuff ain't cheap. We must also factor in the opportunity cost of what we're *not* doing by saying yes to something else. Saying yes to a competitive sports team means saying no to family meals and down time over the weekend. Saying yes to a volunteer role in the classroom or church means saying no to slow morning chats over coffee and cocoa (organic, of course). Saying yes to multiple after-school classes means saying no to home-cooked meals and snuggle breaks after school. (Drs. Neufeld and Maté refer to these snuggles as "collecting" your child after time apart, a key ritual in secure attachment.) Finally, saying yes to all things kid-centric also precludes children from taking on meaningful work at home, which provides immense value to the budding individual and the household alike.

If this sounds positively Grinchy to you, let me put it another way: How often do you really own your yeses? Owning your yes means not only are you willing, but you're looking forward to it and you're willing to sacrifice something to be there. Agreeing to a commitment out of guilt or coercion is not an owned yes.

We only have twenty-four hours in a day, all of us. We can budget those hours as we see fit, but every expenditure depletes from our limited supply of hours. Don't let yourself get to the bottom of the purse, only to realize you are fresh out of hours and haven't yet set aside your daily allowance for rest and reconnection with your family. Rarely are we missed elsewhere, but we are irreplaceable at home.

What I'm advocating for isn't a total rejection of anything outside the home, especially given that neighborhoods in which kids self-organize for hours of free play are hard to come by any more as we sprawl our communities and collectively turn inward, often plugged in and tuned out. Spending time in organized events and classes may be very strategic to accomplish the ends we're targeting for our zones.

But we have to start with a scaffolding of our schedules that allows for downtime, for white space, for the whole family. Make room for nothing! For many families, this means pulling everything off the calendar to force a reset of sorts, seeing what we miss, what we don't, and ensuring our zones are firmly in place before adding in scheduled activities.

Dr. Stixrud and Mr. Johnson frame this in *The Self-Driven Child*: "Start by mapping out the number of hours they need to sleep, how much time they want to spend on sports or other nontech leisure activities, and how much time they need to spend on schoolwork, dinner, chores, or getting ready for school or bed." While they're specifically talking about backing into tech time, the model generally encourages anchoring your priorities firmly in the forefront, and planning the negotiable, non-zone commitments around them.

I grew up with incredible parents who worked full time at our family businesses. Mom co-chaired the PTA and baked muffins for neighbors; Dad parked cars at church on Sunday morning and coached my brother's sports teams. We had plenty on our plates, but I always remember having time to sit in my room and read, play school with my stuffies, make up dance routines on the front porch, or play Army men in the backyard flower bed with my younger brother. I took dance classes, and my brother was on a baseball team before transitioning to hockey (which he still plays today). We had plenty going on, folks.

But here's the kicker: This was all very organic. My parents didn't suggest the activities; we did. If we wanted to try dance and art and karate, we had to pick one at a time, in part because they couldn't play taxi while running two businesses. Some days after school, we had to go to work with them and help around our machine shop, sweeping up shards of metal or making a fresh pot of coffee for the machinists.

We probably stayed busier than my parents could manage, to be honest, but we never felt pressure to perform or engage. And we frequently heard "No." When I quit dance at age twelve, I spent the majority of my time after school reading in my room and trying my best to ride out puberty. Even with college looming on the horizon, I wasn't pressured to add activities to my resume. I was given the space to just be, to rest, and to learn some practical things around the house—like preparing dinner, cleaning house, and caring for the dog—because I was home with time to spare. These have value, too, and I suspect they're overlooked today in the race for college admissions.

Young kids need you to budget on their behalf. And you can't simply budget as though they're mini versions of you or other adults. They have different needs than you and I. They need space, they need play, they need rest, and they need time away from adults. Children must be provided room to create their own domain, to call the shots, and to exercise social skills and movement with others to learn the limits of their behaviors and their bodies.

As they mature, kids also need expectations in terms of contributing around the house, something that will be incredibly difficult to enforce if they're buried in homework or activities every waking hour outside of school. Overly-structuring their hours with simulations of play (dance, music lessons, sports, art classes, educational computer games) or simulations of responsibility (holding them accountable only for attending school and getting high marks) doesn't accomplish the same vital tasks as does unstructured free play and meaningful chores. It's false empowerment that doesn't translate to the real world, which is ultimately where our kids need to thrive without us.

We not only need to ensure that our kids have a solid zone for play, but it needs to be protected, sacrosanct, and it must constitute a good portion of their daily budget. If this is not the norm at the moment for your family, expect a period of adjustment and some pushback. Your kids may whine about chores or writhe at the idea of not being entertained. Of course they will; they're out of practice! But that doesn't mean you throw in the towel. Persist in your efforts to recalibrate your calendar and reorganize your hours, and know that you're investing in a strategy that has tremendous returns.

LEARNING THROUGH PLAY

Treat play as though it is your child's equivalent of work. For many children, the majority of their day is spoken for with school, so education is often considered their "job." This is unfortunate, but I realize not everyone is in a position to homeschool or choose another learning mechanism that doesn't require so many hours in a classroom.

If your child attends school for most of the day, do your best with the hours left to provide protected, prioritized time to play. Push back on homework or overtime so commonly asked of young children. Honor this valuable work time set aside for play—just as you would for a meeting or deadline for your job—and you will make a tremendous investment in this zone and in the future well-being of your offspring.

If you're doing the math, honoring after-school time for unstructured play (meaning kid-led, adult-free, open play) while also trying to implement more family dinners and smoother bedtime routines, that doesn't leave a lot of time for running amuck to classes and practices. That's kind of the point. Take a hard look at your current family schedule (on a physical calendar, if possible), even if just for a week, and calculate how much free time your children have.

I'm not talking about simply the time they're home between school, activities, and bed. Look at how much time is truly *theirs* for playing, creating, and resting. Do they have several hours per day during the week that you'd consider play time? Parking in front of a gaming console or tablet doesn't count here.

For many of us, the answer is no. Do not beat yourself up! We have to actively schedule ourselves out of this, because it's incredibly easy to let months or even years pass without realizing that our kids don't really have time to just *play*. The mere presence of even the most awesome, open-ended toys and materials does not beget an abundance of play. Time does, and we have to make that time in our households and then fiercely protect it.

As *Wild + Free* founder Ainsley Arment puts it, "The trouble with our modern version of childhood is that it strongly resembles the lifestyle of adults and comes at the expense of play. It takes a conscientious community to restore childhood to its original condition, which means sabotaging our selfish ambition, slowing down our children's early education, and restoring play to its central role in their lives." We are that conscientious community of which she speaks, and the importance of this zone cannot be overstated.

Forsaking play is forsaking childhood. And not just the idyllic version that many of us knew in the '80s and '90s, pre-devices in every pocket and backpack. But true, necessary child development doesn't happen in absence of play. On the contrary, ample opportunity for play provides exponential benefits, including—get ready for irony—a child's ability to learn! We're competing with school for the majority of waking hours in our kids' days, recess is on the verge of extinction, and yet play is the optimal means of learning for young children.

A November 2022 article from *The Hechinger Report*, a nonprofit newsroom focused on education advocacy, reported, "Play should not be seen as tangential to learning, experts say, but should be viewed instead as the natural way young children learn."

Childhood education professor Dee Ray was quoted in the article, saying, "The parts of the brain that are most developed in the early years are the ones that respond to active experiences. The brain is structured to learn from experience first, and then learn through all the other means that we usually use [to teach]. Play is essential to education. Play is education for children."

The typical lecture (including video lecture) format leveraged in most schools is better suited for older children who have already developed those aspects of their brains needed for such teaching via experiential learning. We have to meet kids where they are, and what they want and need in those early years is ample doses of play and hands-on experience.

Adults tend to think of play as separate from learning, but that simply isn't true. Play is the means by which children learn. And we're not just talking about school subjects. In child-led play, kids can experiment with social behaviors and feedback with other children (ideally a mix of ages), they can test the limits of their physical strength and build upon it, and they can interact with the physical world to better understand it but also to marvel at it. We can't take the marveling piece for granted, as that is one of the most valuable gifts of childhood. As we get older, the wonder tends to wane. Or rather, it's trained out of us.

CREATIVITY CRAVES SPACE

Children are some of the best innovators and creative thinkers imaginable, and this is true in their natural, organic state. They're natural scientists and inventors. But it's not a given that they'll continue this way. So while we don't have to teach it, we absolutely must protect it.

Creativity expert and psychologist Dr. Robert J. Sternberg explains, "Creativity is a habit. The problem is that schools sometimes treat it as a bad habit.... Like any habit, creativity can either be encouraged or discouraged." I like to think of creativity as wonder made actionable, turning an observation or curiosity into an experiment or harnessing inspiration into another form.

Tony Wagner's book *Creating Innovators: The Making of Young People Who Will Change the World* is a wonderful study in innovators of all sorts, those who haven't had their creativity taught out of them. He observes that some of the childhood variables contributing to innovative minds into adulthood are: plenty of free, unstructured play; prioritizing sleep; open communication with parents who listen; boredom; practical expectations (chores and responsibilities); room to explore (physically and mentally); and hands-on experience. Sound familiar?

Our current conveyor belt of kids-as-products removes space for wonder and for intrinsic motivation to drive. As Wagner puts it, "It shocks me the number of young people who have no idea what they are interested in because they have been pushed to achieve versus pushed to explore."

Kids need time to unfold as unique individuals, who see the world in specific, valuable ways. They need space to observe their environment and decide what problems they want to solve, and who they want to serve. Running from class to class, appointment to appointment, playdate to playdate, doesn't provide the kind of white space to consider their role in the bigger picture. And kids need that. We need that, too.

The future is unknown. What skills or jobs will be relevant in forty years is undetermined. Technology such as Artificial

Intelligence is changing industries and occupations even as I type this, so the idea that we can keep plugging away at the same pace, leveraging the same strategies we've been using for seventy years without adaptation, is simply foolish.

We have to target different outcomes, not only for academics, but in terms of well-being and emotional intelligence for our children (both of which are bolstered in play). Our kids are going to need to adapt in ways that current curriculum and trends don't support.

Wagner teamed up with Ted Dintersmith to write *Most Likely to Succeed: Preparing Our Kids for the Innovation Era*, and they put it bluntly: "If you want to get inspired about our country's future, look to our innovators, our social entrepreneurs, our start-ups. And if you want to get discouraged, look at how we educate our kids.... We micromanage every lesson plan. Instead of letting a thousand flowers bloom, we replace all the flowers with the same lifeless, overtested weed."

This isn't a diatribe against schools or formal education. It is, however, a reminder that we need to fight for ample time for our children to play and to explore. We have to plan our homes and our family schedules to allow for white space to create and to wonder. Public education doesn't do this for us. In fact, it requires a lot of unwinding after school—a whole zone, really—to set the stage for the kind of thinking and playing that helps young minds develop and unfold as needed for their flourishing.

We need what your unique children have to offer. We need their ideas, their passions, their solutions, and their creativity. Don't let them pass through like everyone else. They're not a product. Children are not commodities.

These are our children. Our immensely valuable children.

GET IN THE ZONE

- Examine your family schedule—does your child have several hours *per day* to play?
- Consider where you can create buffer zones from structure (cancel or say no to something)
- Push back on homework and excess extracurriculars and invites
- Get out of the way... let them take the lead when it comes to play
- Engage children in meaningful work in the home
- Treat play like your child's most important work
- Protect wonder and creativity

CROSSING GUARDS

- Deborah MacNamara, PhD — *Rest, Play, Grow: Making Sense of Preschoolers (Or Anyone Who Acts Like One)*
- Kim John Payne, MED and Lisa M. Ross — *Simplicity Parenting: Using the Extraordinary Power of Less to Raise Calmer, Happier, and More Secure Kids*
- Tony Wagner — *Creating Innovators: The Making of Young People Who Will Change the World*
- Tony Wagner and Ted Dintersmith — *Most Likely to Succeed: Preparing Our Kids for the Innovation Era*
- William Stixrud, PhD and Ned Johnson — *The Self-Driven Child: The Science and Sense of Giving Your Kids More Control Over Their Lives*

Chapter 6

THE STUFF PROBLEM

No one ever tells you that becoming a parent means you'll soon share a home with any number of collections. Outside things become inside things as rocks, sticks, and pinecones are gathered and cherished as part of a beloved bevy of *things*.

No matter how many times you try to slyly move the outside things back outside, they're discovered and promptly relocated to their rightful place inside—in a closet, on a window sill, or proudly displayed on the bar counter forever and ever, amen—usually with at least one scoff of disbelief that you would even consider breaking up the collection. If your entryway resembles scenery from the *Blair Witch Project*, know that you're in good company.

I lead in jest our discussion about stuff because I know this is yet another really valuable zone that can be tough to navigate. Some of us were raised by hoarders and hate all things material (it's me), while others had scant physical memories and therefore hold on to every single thing forever. Some of us can't stop buying presents and toys for our kids at every turn, while others are battling someone else infusing stuff into our homes. (Grandparents, we're coming for ya!) Some of our kids value everything so dearly that the idea of decluttering is cause for panic, while others are ruthless in their willingness to discard even the most sentimental of items.

People orient toward stuff very differently, and that's OK. We can't expect everyone to feel the same way about physical possessions, nor can we as parents and caregivers exert too much force out of our own preferences here. When you're part of a family, you share space, and that should be honored.

We do, however, hold a very valuable role in cultivating not only the physical environment for our homes but also our children's attitudes when it comes to things. What comes into our homes can directly impact our physical and mental health, so we should take this aspect of parenting pretty seriously. Yet it's an area that's often overlooked and certainly not discussed.

Or rather, a bent toward consumerism is the default, with toys abounding and noisy objects spilling into every room of the home, a child never without a play thing. But there are aspects of this norm that we must yet again pump the brakes on to consider what is best for our children and for our families. I am not about to tell you to toss out every last stuffie or make you feel guilty for ample presents at birthdays or holidays. (As I write this, our Christmas tree is lined with many beautiful gifts for each child, and I have zero qualms about that.) But we are certainly going to consider the stuff that surrounds our children and ensure that we're as mindful about it as we are every other aspect we've discussed thus far.

It does matter, turns out, what kind of stuff we have in our home around our kids, so let's ensure we don't subscribe to a default that we never formally considered.

PHYSICAL SPACE IMPACTS MENTAL SPACE

Do you remember when Marie Kondo came onto the scene in 2010, and her KonMari Method was all the rage? We went room to room, speaking to our belongings, asking if they "sparked joy" and organizing whatever was deemed joyful and keep-worthy into carefully folded parcels, ideally in rainbow order. (To be fair, I still organize my closet in rainbow order. It is actually quite pleasing, not going to lie. Joy sparked.)

Or perhaps you're younger (ahem) and you're hooked on *The Home Edit*, pouring over beautiful organization and display ideas for every corner and facet of your home. If you're anything like me, upon looking at these designed spaces you often wonder, *Ok, but where is all the crap? No way anyone actually lives there.*

Remember the priceless collections we led this chapter with? I don't see those in the gorgeously arranged children's closet or play areas, nor do I see the Lego dragon missing a wing or the bent slinky from the preschool treasure box that just doesn't slink anymore.

While these organizational movements and the beautiful images inspired by them can make us chuckle at their lack of real-life "styling"—a la dirty footprints on the rug and rocks on the dinner table—they do remind us that enhancing and managing our environment can have an impact on how we feel and function in that space.

Aesthetically pleasing and efficiently organized areas of the home can change how we feel—and the converse is also true. Just thinking about having to get into my laundry room cabinets to fish out a rarely used gadget or product makes me cringe, anticipating disorganized chaos, items inevitably falling out of said cabinet, and probably saying a few mouth-washed-out-with-soap words while

I'm at it. The reality is that physical clutter results in mental clutter. Stuff strewn about and occupying every corner of every room takes its toll on us, even if you're not a Type-A mama like me.

According to an article from *The Royal Australian College of General Practitioners*, "Clutter can make us feel stressed, anxious and depressed. Research from the United States in 2009, for instance, found the levels of the stress hormone cortisol were higher in mothers whose home environment was cluttered. A chronically cluttered home environment can lead to a constant low-grade fight-or-flight response, taxing our resources designed for survival."

Many of us hear statistics and reports like these, especially as they've become more visible, and assume the answer is to organize. Grab some matching baskets, bust out the label maker, and bring order to the chaos of crap. But organizing and tidying is simply moving around the same volume of stuff; in fact, we add stuff—organization supplies like baskets and bins—to manage our stuff!

Coming at the stuff problem from the perspective of a parent or caregiver is especially important because in addition to the general impact of the overabundance of things, we are specifically impacted in our response as caregivers. A 2021 study published in the journal *Comprehensive Psychoneuroendocrinology* found that chaotic household environments—modeled in the study via toys and clutter strewn about in view, TV or music on in the background, and reducing the perceived size of the room— increased the physiological stress (measured via saliva sample) in a simulated caregiving context.

What's interesting is that only the objective data (saliva sample) reflected this stress response; the subjects did not self-report a difference in stress while caregiving in a messy versus a tidy environment. We aren't even consciously aware of how our environment is impacting how we show up as parents, but it sure as heck is.

In my research on clutter and how it impacts our mental and physical state, the key is that the problem is overabundance. No one is advocating for stark, sparsely filled spaces. That hardly sounds like home, especially when it comes to raising kids; they come with stuff. We share our homes with our families, and everyone comes with stuff.

The problem is *too much* stuff. I don't think anyone sets out to own a bunch of crap or fill their closets and cubbies with junk. But it's very culturally normal to acquire heaps of possessions and to just move them from place to place... forever and ever, amen.

Moving the needle on alleviating your physical clutter to benefit your mental experience requires decluttering, or as minimalism expert Joshua Becker calls it, *de-owning*. Removing items from your home is what will ultimately create the kind of change that we need, whether we know it or not. The great news is that we'll examine the less-crap zone from several different angles, and we'll see that all of them reinforce the need for fewer things, and for mindfulness around the things that make their way into our homes.

TOYS THAT INSPIRE

Given that our focus for creating these zones is ensuring that our children can thrive and develop as optimally as possible, we can't help but touch on toys. We've learned in general the benefits of keeping our whole home free from clutter (not just hiding it), but sometimes those bedrooms and playrooms can feel like black holes.

Maybe you're like many parents who keep the majority of the house tidy and orderly, but it looks like a plastic rainbow bomb blew up upon entering the kids' rooms. Or perhaps the room is presentable, but God forbid the closet is opened and Pandora herself bursts forth, surrounded by toys and dolls and things that make such a racket, you'll wonder why the inventors so hate parents.

Our children are also highly susceptible to their environments, so we cannot give a pass to their spaces any more than we can our own. In following some of the advice I'm about to share, I've found that my children are often more engaged with and interested in their toys when we've streamlined, and spend more time in their rooms, occupied and playing contently as space is made. There's fruit in doing the work of decluttering, and I promise it doesn't have to be painful. In fact, it's incredibly freeing.

The prevailing recommendations when it comes to toys is to focus on fewer but better. This is actually solid advice where anything is concerned, especially if you're trying to reduce the number of things you own. Regarding toys specifically, offering high-quality, open-ended options means your kids can play with them in many ways, for many years.

Open-ended toys are those that can be used in many different ways, versus toys that are "fixed" and can be used in a singular manner. Think about the classics, like blocks, magnetic tiles, modular building systems (like Legos), dress-up clothes, figurines, play silks, dolls, and stuffies. These allow your child to infuse their own creative ideas into the toys, reusing them in various different ways to encourage hours of self-directed play.

Opting for longer-lasting materials such as wood and steel, and avoiding cheap plastic, ensures you're not creating more waste with repeated play and that beloved staples can hang around for years. Knowing a toy will survive several children (i.e., "heirloom quality") is a great litmus test for whether to bring it into your home or add it to the wish list.

Plastic toys that emit noise and lights may seem fun and are often marketed as educational to boot, but these are often fixed (meaning they don't lend themselves to being reimagined as other things or for other uses) and are prone to breaking. When a toy has broken or a set is incomplete, children will rarely re-engage with it. This is a good candidate for the trash bin, but we don't necessarily want to get in the habit of destining toys for the landfill after a brief period of play. Invest in what will last and what will also feed your child's creative instincts.

If you're finding that your young child is constantly coming out of free play time in their room or playroom whining with discontentment, there's a chance they may have too many fixed toys and not enough open-ended items to dive into. You can also set out a few items or materials and ask, "What shall we create today?" Stick around to help them engage, but don't direct their play, and once they take off, you're free to move on.

Going back to the mental overwhelm of stuff, even an abundance of solid, open-ended toys is too much. The volume of toys can create a mental block that keeps children from engaging with what they have, so ensure there is white space on the ground to play, counters clear, and a rotation of fantastic toys or sets on display to help cultivate a space that just begs for hours of imaginative play.

We revisit *Simplicity Parenting*, where Kim John Payne advises, "A smaller, more manageable quantity of toys invites deeper play and engagement. An avalanche of toys invites emotional disconnect and a sense of overwhelm." (There is a whole chapter about environment in this book, and it's a great deep dive into establishing a space for children to thrive.)

I've seen my kids in playrooms with a remarkable volume of toys and while they're excited at first, I watch them buzz through items, grabbing something, playing with it for a few moments, and then tossing it aside for the next. They never actually engage with anything (though making a proper mess) and inevitably show signs of irritability and discontentment sooner than their norm. The fun is very short-lived.

Just as we covered in our media chapter, one of the most powerful feedback mechanisms you have here is watching your own kid. Especially with teens, pay attention to what successfully gets them off screens for a bit. Is it physical play like a climbing gym or obstacle course? Consider how you can bring these elements into your home and provide materials to encourage this type of play.

Do you notice that your little one loves to build or create worlds with blocks and tiles? Provide a variety of building materials and figurines to spur on their creativity and innovation. Children have natural proclivities, so don't assume that every toy must-have is going to guarantee a slam dunk in delivering satisfaction. I like to look for quality materials secondhand to see what takes and what doesn't. When something doesn't seem to get a lot of attention, we donate or sell it to another family to keep the cognitive load of playthings in check.

I talked about avoiding the pitfalls of organizing versus decluttering, but that doesn't mean that you shouldn't organize what you have. Keep the space orderly and ensure everything has a place. This is the best way to create a system in which your kids can (and do) clean up. If my kiddos want to watch a show for a bit, we first ensure that we've had plenty of play, and that we've tidied up from said play.

This takes only moments because we know where everything goes, and the system generally sticks unless we've introduced a bunch of new stuff (think birthdays or Christmas). These are good opportunities to revisit what we have, find a home for everything, and let them own that space. Especially for sets with lots of small things, like Barbie dolls and accessories, grab some bins or baskets to keep everything in one place. (Have you noticed that toys designed for girls come with a thousand little parts? It's madness.) Keeping Legos, building blocks, or Play-Doh supplies in bins also makes it easy to pull out the set as a means of encouraging play when they're struggling to dive in. (It happens. We all find ourselves wanting to be passively entertained at times. Give a little nudge and it goes a long way.)

DRAMA-FREE DECLUTTERING

As I mentioned earlier, we all bring different baggage with us (pun intended) when it comes to stuff and possessions. Given that getting rid of things can be really tough for some—and a little too easy for others (looking at you, rage cleaners)—it's worth taking a moment to consider some ways that this can go down with less fuss, resulting in greater success long-term. Remember, we want to establish zones that not only benefit them as kids, but that they can also carry with them into adulthood. Children are natural hoarders with little self-control, so we have to help them grow out of that tendency.

Joshua Becker, author of *The More of Less: Finding the Life You Want Under Everything You Own*, reinforces the need for zones by warning, "Children who do not learn to set boundaries for themselves too often become adults who do not set boundaries for themselves." We should expect kids to be kids, constantly craving novelty and newness... and our kids should expect us to love them enough to train them in self-control and delayed gratification. (Remember the Marshmallow Experiment from our media discussion?)

I've read conflicting advice in terms of whether we ought to include our children in the decluttering process. I think a lot of this comes down to the kid. If she's going to emphatically insist on keeping the single piece of confetti from the birthday party four years ago, or that the action figure missing limbs is vital to his collection, you may want to do this on your own. When my children have been in those phases, I thin out their toys without them, but hang onto items they may ask about for about a month. (My son is the type who remembers a paper airplane he made four months ago.) Beyond that, they get tossed or donated.

However, my children are now eight and four years old, so we declutter together. I usually provide some parameters around how we can wisely decide what to keep, what gets donated, and what gets thrown away.

For example, broken things go in the garbage, toys we've outgrown but still work get donated/passed down, toys we forgot about and haven't missed may be ready for a new home, etc. Start with clothes they've outgrown or another category of stuff that isn't as loaded for your kids. You can develop your own rubric to align with your family values, but the key is to collaborate and to make a solid dent. Removing two things from a room of stuff hardly counts as decluttering.

Choosing your moments for decluttering with your family is important, too. I like to use upcoming birthdays and holidays like Christmas to encourage a purge. With the anticipation of imminent new additions, you practically need to create room for those items anyway. And kids are more likely to get on board when they know they aren't going without. Also, if your kids are tired or cranky, choose another time to do this. If *you* are tired and cranky, don't do it. We get trash-happy when we're off our game, so just wait.

Without exception, every time I've followed this framework—setting guidelines, inviting the kids to be part of the process, and planning a purge before we expect some new additions, when everyone is in good spirits—my kids leave the experience content and usually dive into their remaining toys for a solid play session. And I can't even tell you what a weight I feel lifted to see some white space in the cubbies and closet.

Less really is more.

GROWING GRACEFUL CONSUMERS

Managing this zone, like others, is unfortunately not a one-and-done. It takes ongoing effort and mindfulness to keep stuff at bay and to protect your home environment. Decluttering is an awesome starting point for where you are today, but if you're finding the need to declutter on a regular basis, the problem may be what comes *into* your space. Keeping the guidelines for what is worthy of hanging onto in mind when you're shopping and creating wish lists for the kids allows you to break the habit of having so many toss-worthy items with which to contend.

This is also a great opportunity to share your approach to toys and gifts for your children with loved ones who may be frequent gift givers. It is not rude to ask family members and friends to refrain from introducing fixed items or noisy, battery-operated toys into your home, especially given those rarely last. (I don't know many people who would be pleased knowing their gift is rarely used or breaks shortly after giving.) We often create and share wish lists for holidays and birthdays to help target certain additions to our repertoire, but we're also not afraid to come out and request experiences, seasonal clothes, or other practical items as well. Approach this with humility and honesty, and you'll save yourself a lot of drama and work down the road.

Speaking of giving, dealing with the stuff problem is a natural opportunity to discuss generosity with your children. It may be in the context of donating toys to local shelters or children's homes or of choosing a child from an Angel Tree or Salvation Army gift drive. We may simply take some time mid-declutter to remark on how blessed we are to see so many beautiful toys and to think of how many hours of enjoyment they've provided... and may provide to others.

We don't want to raise children who are constantly situated in the center of their universe, so connecting moments like these to a bigger picture, to others in need or want, is important for cultivating gratefulness, empathy, and perspective beyond their own desires.

The other benefit of coaching your child through their relationship with stuff is that you can reinforce this perspective with every trip to the store or looking over your shoulder as you shop online. Targeting less-but-better and keeping needs versus desires as part of the conversation are values that will benefit your child into adulthood and support development of healthy relationships with things. We don't want our kids to be just another consumer, ever longing for more new things. This will not satisfy, and the perpetually unmet desire can manifest as increasingly problematic behaviors down the line, such as addiction and excess debt.

Help them learn the importance of saving, giving, and spending so that they understand that things cost something. Use some of that meaningful work around the home we've discussed to fund an allowance or savings account so they can budget for their own toys and gadgets, as well as their own generosity.

We are always, always, always playing the long game here. Paving a zone in which our children are relieved of clutter, healthily oriented toward to their belongings, inspired by the toys and materials in their rooms, and bent toward generosity and contentment, we will prepare our children for a bright future in which they aren't going broke or miserable trying to keep up with the Joneses. This is a legacy of freedom.

GET IN THE ZONE

- Recognize that your physical environment impacts your mental space
- Don't just tidy and organize... get rid of it!
- Your new toy mantra: less but better
- Set guidelines for decluttering and decide to keep, toss, or donate/sell
- Choose your moment for decluttering when you're all up for it
- Respectfully share your journey and communicate your toy preferences to gift givers
- Reinforce the importance of gratitude and generosity with your children

- Apply these guidelines when shopping to reduce cluttering inputs
- Coach your children in needs versus wants
- Help children connect value and work to things

CROSSING GUARDS

- Joshua Becker — *The More of Less: Finding the Life You Want Under Everything You Own* and *BecomingMinimalist. com*
- Kim John Payne, MED and Lisa M. Ross — *Simplicity Parenting: Using the Extraordinary Power of Less to Raise Calmer, Happier, and More Secure Kids*
- Simone Davies — *The Montessori Toddler: A Parent's Guide to Raising a Curious and Responsible Human Being*

Conclusion

YOU GOT THIS!

This parenting gig doesn't come with instructions. There is no playbook for caregivers to get through child-rearing unscathed. We're all learning on the job. But this is the most important job there is, so it's vital that we give ourselves and each other a ton of grace and encouragement, and that we never stop learning or trying to stay ahead of the curve. *The School Zone Mentality* is about living out a framework for us, as child-raisers, that ignores what is common and embraces what is better according to modern insights from science and specialists.

We're going to focus on providing food that fuels our bodies and supports young minds. And we're going to help them stay well and fit for wherever life takes them. We'll bring whole foods to the forefront and inspire others with balanced lunches that our littles helped pack. Then we'll get incredible nights of sleep with habits that strengthen circadian rhythms, propelling kids into their days ready to learn, focus, and explore. Built in pressure values will naturally reduce the bedtime burden, equipping our kids to self-regulate in their own special way. They'll also learn to choose devices and media more carefully based on your leadership when it comes to mindful media. We will be the families that prioritize real connections, in person, and that build communities where delayed smartphone ownership is encouraged.

Say it with me: "We will let them play!" Honor the wiggles and make room for nothing... which is actually everything. And let us create spaces that leave room for innovation, creativity, and visual ease. This is the childhood our kids truly need, and we're going to fight to give it to them.

I've spent almost ten years now reading everything I could get my hands on when it comes to parenting, child development, neuroscience, and health and wellness. There is still so much to learn and discover, but I'm motivated to keep pursuing based on how these insights have informed my parenting and transformed our family already.

I love being in the trenches right alongside you. I envision a world in which our children are honored, their littleness respected, their well-being protected, and where we sow seeds daily in preparation for their eventual departure from our homes as whole, healthy, motivated individuals. And if we've done our jobs well, our "bigs" will take their places in the world and pave their very own zones for their families, utilizing the latest and greatest information that has yet to be discovered.

We've done some incredible work here together, creating awareness of cultural norms that are diminishing the capacities of our children and impairing our communities as a result. We need each other, and when kids are treated like mini-adults instead of the emerging humans that they are, we stunt our ability to thrive as families, neighborhoods, and villages.

By establishing some (or all, you beautiful overachievers) of the zones in this book, you are stepping out of the status quo and into a lifestyle that declares that our kids need something different from what they're currently being offered. Kids don't have to be anxious, selfish, unmotivated, overweight, lonely, and overwhelmed.

We can truly change that traffic pattern. We cannot treat our babies as the priceless canaries in the coal mines. We have the wake-up call of a lifetime to see that we are not OK when our kids are not OK. And they're not OK. Not by a long shot. Things are getting worse year over year, but we're heeding the signals and pumping the brakes.

Better yet, let's slam on those brakes. Enough is enough. You've made it this far, and you now have knowledge and strategies you can employ to counter the status quo. These changes take time, and the work takes heart, but you are perfectly positioned to protect your family. We must slow down to consider how we're raising children, and you've done just that by taking the time to explore these zones and why they matter!

Changing the way your family eats, the way they sleep, what they watch/hear, how they spend time, and what they own—upholding developmentally critical zones—is an investment that is a legacy all its own. Paving these zones for your children is your high calling as a parent, caregiver, or anyone else reading this book who loves a child.

I have no doubt that there are many additional zones that would serve our kids, and now that you've nearly finished this book, you can spot those opportunities in your own home. As I've mentioned, paying attention to *your* own kids, going into scientist mode, is going to be the most impactful means of diverting traffic destined for dead ends. You know your child better than anyone, and recognizing where they need support most urgently—be it the zones we covered in the previous chapters or others—is key for securing their safety and well-being.

And then take it a step further: Share your successes (without embarrassing or violating trust, of course) with other parents and loved ones to enrich your inner circle and cultivate the village we so desperately need to honor raising children, letting others know that they're not alone in wanting something different for these generations. Get behind the wheel and honk loudly, refusing to sit idly, and bring others alongside you. Ignore those doubts and fears, and boldly proclaim a different path for your nearest and dearest.

No matter how many incredible parents I talk to over the years—from my mother-in-law who raised four kids, to my eighty-year-old Mamaw who has outlived grandchildren but never lost her spark—they all admit that they have no idea what they're doing. They figure it out as they go, they learn from their mistakes, and they never stop learning. Take notes from the closest thing we have to a playbook—these wise, experienced parents—and don't stop making these pursuits a priority. Keep learning, allow yourself to change your mind, and stay open. But *go*.

One of the most important things I can leave you with is this: You're the parent. No one else can raise your children. Own your role as their parent. Don't try to be their friend. (Go back to Chapter 1 if you need another pep talk.) If you don't raise them, culture will, and as we've seen, it's a lousy teacher. Don't underestimate their resilience or ability to understand what's important.

Children are *incredible*. My son and daughter never cease to amaze me, and I can't wait to see how they impact the world with their gifts and talents. My job is to help them unfold fully in an environment of safety, growth, and respect. These zones have been pivotal in our home, and I pray they are for yours as well.

REFERENCES

CHAPTER 1: PRIMED FOR CHANGE

Clear, James. *Atomic Habits: An Easy & Proven way to Build Good Habits & Break Bad Ones.* (Avery, 2018).

Grant, Adam. (@AdamMGrant). "Refusing to change your mind is a decision to stop learning." Twitter, now X. September 2, 2022. https://x.com/AdamMGrant/status/1565730168261443587.

Postman, Neil. *Building a Bridge to the 18th Century: How the Past Can Improve Our Future.* (Alfred A. Knopf, 1999).

CHAPTER 2: FOOD IS FUEL

Akagawa, Shohei, Yuko Akagawa, Sohsaku Yamanouchi, Takahisa Kimata, Shoji Tsuji, Kazunari Kaneko. "Development of the Gut Microbiota and Dysbiosis in Children." *Bioscience of Microbiota Food and Health* vol. 40 no. 1 (August 24, 2020): 12–18.

CDC. *Obesity.* "Childhood Obesity Facts." 2024. https://www.cdc.gov/obesity/childhood-obesity-facts/childhood-obesity-facts.html. Accessed 2024.

CDC. *Managing Health Conditions in School.* "Food Allergies in Schools." https://www.cdc.gov/school-health-conditions/food-allergies/. Accessed 2024.

Chacón C, Arteaga I, Martínez-Escudé A, Ruiz Rojano I, Lamonja-Vicente N, Caballeria L, Ribatallada Diez AM, Schröder H, Montraveta M, Bovo MV, Ginés P, Pera G, Diez-Fadrique G, Pachón-Camacho A, Alonso N, Graupera I, Torán-Monserrat P, Expósito C. "Clinical epidemiology of non-alcoholic fatty liver disease in children and adolescents." The LiverKids: Study protocol. *PLoS One.* 2023 Oct 13;18(10):e0286586. doi: 10.1371/journal.pone.0286586. PMID: 37831682; PMCID: PMC10575486.

Children's Health. *Fatty liver disease in children is on the rise.* https://www.childrens.com/health-wellness/fatty-liver-disease-in-children-on-the-rise. Accessed 2024.

Fulkerson, Jayne A, Mary Story, Alison Mellin, Nancy Leffert, Dianne Neumark-Sztainer, Simone A. French. Family Dinner Meal Frequency and Adolescent Development: Relationships with Developmental Assets and High-Risk Behaviors. *Journal of Adolescent Health*, vol. 39 no. 3 (June 30, 2006): 337–345.

Macmillan, Carrie. "Ultraprocessed Foods: Are They Bad for You?" *Yale Medicine.org*. (July 10, 2024). https://www.yalemedicine.org/news/ultraprocessed-foods-bad-for-you.

Means, Casey, MD. *Good Energy: The Surprising Connection between Metabolism and Limitless Health*. (Avery, 2024).

Neumark-Sztainer, Dianne, Melanie Wall, Mary Story, Jayne A. Fulkerson. "Are Family Meal Patterns Associated with Disordered Eating Behaviors Among Adolescents?" *Journal of Adolescent Health* vol. 35 no. 5 (November 2004): 350-359.

Santos, Gabriela Carvalho Jurerna, Matheus Santos de Sousa Fernandes, Pacheco Gabriela Carniel, Anderson da Silva Garcêz, Caral Góis Leandro l, Raquel Canuto. "Dietary Intake in Children and Adolescents with Food Addiction: A Systematic Review." *Addictive Behaviors Reports* vol 19 (June 2024).

Tsoi, Man-Fung, Hang-Long Li, Qi Feng, Ching-Lung Cheung, Tommy T. Cheung, Bernard M. Y. Cheung. "Prevalence of Childhood Obesity in the United States in 1999-2018: A 20-Year Analysis." *Obesity Facts: The European Journal of Obesity* vol 15 issue 4 (August. 2022): 560-569.

CHAPTER 3: SUPERPOWERED SLEEP

American Academy of Child and Adolescent Psychiatry. *Caffeine and Children*. 2020. https://www.aacap.org/AACAP/Families_and_Youth/Facts_for_Families/FFF-Guide/Caffeine_and_Children-131.aspx. Accessed 2024.

American Sleep Apnea Association. *The State of Sleep Health in America 2023.* https://www.sleephealth.org/sleep-health/ the-state-of-sleephealth-in-america/ Accessed 2024.

British Association of Perinatal Medicine. "9 in 10 parents co-sleep but less than half know how to reduce the risk of SIDS." 2023. https://www.bapm.org/articles/9-in-10-parents-co-sleep- but-less-than-half-know-how-to-reduce-the-risk-of-sids. Accessed 2024.

Carter, Ben, Philippa Rees, Lauren Hale, Darsharna Bhattacharjee, Mandar S. Paradkar. "Association Between Portable Screen-Based Media Device Access or Use and Sleep Outcomes: A Systematic Review and Meta-analysis." *JAMA Pediatrics.* (October 31, 2016).

Crouch, Andy. *The Tech-Wise Family: Everyday Steps for Putting Technology in Its Proper Place.* (Baker Books, 2017).

Finucane, Elaine, Ann O'Brien, Shaun Treweek, John Newell, Kishor Das, Sarah Chapman, Paul Wicks, et al. "Does Reading a Book in Bed Make a Difference to Sleep in Comparison to Not Reading a Book in Bed? The People's Trial-an Online, Pragmatic, Randomised Trial." *BioMed Central* (December 2021).

Harvard Health Publishing. "Blue Light Has a Dark Side." *Harvard Health.* (July 24, 2024). https://www.health.harvard.edu/ staying-healthy/blue-light-has-a-dark-side.

Mayo Clinic Health System. "Sleep: An essential element of success for children." (March 3, 2023). https://www.mayoclinichealthsystem. org/hometown-health/speaking-of-health/ sleep-an-essential-element-of-success-for-children.

National Institute of General Medical Sciences. "Circadian Rhythms." (September 2023). https://www.nigms.nih.

gov/education/fact-sheets/Pages/circadian-rhythms.aspx. Accessed 2025.

Office of Disease Prevention and Health Promotion. "Healthy People 2030." https://odphp.health.gov/healthypeople. Accessed 2024.

Office of Disease Prevention and Health Promotion. "Increase the proportion of children who get sufficient sleep — EMC-03.". *National Survey of Children's Health (NSCH).* https://odphp.health.gov/healthypeople/objectives-and-data/browse-objectives/children/increase-proportion-children-who-get-sufficient-sleep-emc-03. Accessed 2024.

Payton, L'Oreal Thompson. "Here's the exact time you need to go to bed for a good night's sleep, according to science." *Fortune.* (March 13, 2023). https://fortune.com/well/2023/05/13/best-time-to-sleep.

Payne, Kim John, MED, Lisa M. Ross. *Simplicity Parenting: Using the Extraordinary Power of Less to Raise Calmer, Happier, and More Secure Kids.* (Ballantine Books, 2009).

Shepard-Ohta, Rachael. "Proprioception: The Sixth Sense." *Hey, Sleepy Baby.* (May 23, 2022). https://heysleepybaby.com/blog/proprioception-the-sixth-sense.

Stixrud, William, Ned Johnson. *The Self-Driven Child: The Science and Sense of Giving Your Kids More Control Over Their Lives.* (Viking, 2018).

Tkacz Joseph, Brenna L. Brady. "Increasing Rate of Diagnosed Childhood Mental Illness in the United States: Incidence, Prevalence and Costs." *Public Health in Practice* vol. 2 (November 2021).

Wiessinger, Diane, Diana West, Linda J. Smith, Teresa Pitman. "The Safe Sleep Seven." *La Leche League International.* (November 28, 2018). https://llli.org/news/the-safe-sleep-seven/.

Williamson, A. M., Anne-Marie Feyer. "Moderate Sleep Deprivation Produces Impairments in Cognitive and Motor Performance Equivalent to Legally Prescribed Levels of Alcohol Iintoxication." *Occupational & Environmental Medicine* vol 57 issue 10 (October 2000).

CHAPTER 4: MINDFUL MEDIA

Cleveland Clinic. "An Ode to Silence: Why You Need It In Your Life." August 7, 2020. https://health.clevelandclinic.org/why-you-need-more-silence-in-your-life.

Common Sense Media. "How We Rate and Review." https://www.commonsensemedia.org/about-us/our-mission/About-our-ratings. Accessed 2024.

Haidt, Jonathan. *The Anxious Generation: How the Great Rewiring of Childhood Is Causing an Epidemic of Mental Illness.* (Penguin Press, 2024).

Kennedy, Russell, MD. *Anxiety Rx: A New Prescription for Anxiety Relief from the Doctor Who Created It.* (Awaken Village Press, 2020).

Koch, Kathy, PhD. *Screens and Teens: Connecting with Our Kids in a Wireless World.* (Moody Publishers, 2015).

Neufeld, Gordon, PhD, Gabor Maté, MD. *Hold On to Your Kids: Why Parents Need to Matter More than Peers.* (Ballantine Books, 2014).

Ortutay, Barbara, Haleuya Hadero. "Meta, TikTok and other social media CEOs testify in heated Senate hearing on child exploitation." *AP News.* January 31, 2024. https://apnews.com/article/Meta-tiktok-snap-discord-zuckerberg-testify-senate-00754a6bea92aaad62585ed 55f219932.

Ryssdal, Kai, Sarah Leeson, Sean McHenry. "Teens have "kept the economy going," and their workforce numbers show it." *Marketplace.* January 29 2024. https://www.marketplace. org/2024/01/29/teen-workforce-rise/.

Sampson, Eve. "Australia Moves to Ban Young Teens From Social Media." *The New York Times.* November 11, 2024. https:// www.nytimes.com/2024/11/07/world/australia/australia-teens-social-media.html.

Sapien Labs. "Study Out from Sapien Labs Links Age of First Smartphone to Mental Wellbeing." March 14, 2023. https:// sapienlabs.org/whats_new/study-out-from-sapien-labs-links-age-of-first-smartphone-to-mental-wellbeing.

Smith, Nigel. "Christopher Nolan on His Viewing Habits, the 'Hard Job' of Making Films and Why He Doesn't Email." *People.* December 12, 2020. https://people.com/movies/christopher-nolan-viewing-habits-making-movies-not-using-email.

Urban Dictionary. *Alone Together.* https://www.urbandictionary. com/ define.php?term=alone%20together. Accessed 2025.

CHAPTER 5: HONORING THE HOURS

Arment, Ainsley. *The Call of the Wild + Free: Reclaiming Wonder in Your Child's Education.* (Harper One, 2019).

MacNamara, Deborah, PhD. *Rest, Play, Grow: Making Sense of Preschoolers (Or Anyone Who Acts Like One).* (Aona Books, 2016).

Mader, Jackie. "Want resilient and well-adjusted kids? Let them play." *The Hechinger Report.* November 14, 2022. https://hechingerreport.org/want-resilient-and-well-adjusted-kids-let-them-play.

Payne, Kim John, MED, Lisa M. Ross. *Simplicity Parenting: Using the Extraordinary Power of Less to Raise Calmer, Happier, and More Secure Kids.* (Ballantine Books, 2009).

Sternberg, Robert J. "Creativity Is a Habit." *Education Week.* February 21, 2006. http://www.edweek.org/ew/articles/2006/02/22/24sternberg.h25.html.

Stixrud, William, Johnson, Ned. *The Self-Driven Child: The Science and Sense of Giving Your Kids More Control over Their Lives.* (Viking, 2018).

Wagner, Tony. *Creating Innovators: The Making of Young People Who Will Change the World.* (Scriber, 2012).

Wagner, Tony, Ted Dintersmith. *Most Likely to Succeed: Preparing Our Kids for the Innovation Era.* (Scribner, 2016).

CHAPTER 6: THE STUFF PROBLEM

Becker, Joshua. *The More of Less: Finding the Life You Want Under Everything You Own.* (WaterBrook Press, 2016).

Bodrij, F. Fenne, Suzanne M. Andeweg, Mariëlle J. L. Prevoo, Ralph C. A. Rippe, Lenneke R. A. Alink. "The Causal Effect of Household Chaos on Stress and Caregiving: An Experimental Study." *Comprehensive Psychoneuroendocrinology* vol 8 (November 2021).

Payne, Kim John, MED, Lisa M. Ross. *Simplicity Parenting: Using the Extraordinary Power of Less to Raise Calmer, Happier, and More Secure Kids.* (Ballantine Books, 2009).

Sternberg, Robert J. "Creativity Is a Habit." *Education Week*. February 21, 2006. https://www.edweek.org/teaching-learning/opinion-creativity-is-a-habit/2006/02.

Sander, Libby (Elizabeth). "Time for a Kondo clean-out? Here's what clutter does to your brain and body." *The Conversation*. January 20, 2019. https://theconversation.com/time-for-a-kondo-clean-out-heres-what-clutter-does-to-your-brain-and-body-109947.

ACKNOWLEDGMENTS

Asher and Olivia, I am honored that God chose me to be your mommy. Asher, your interest in and support of this book is so special, and I can't wait to see your books on the shelf next to mine. I am proud of who you are. Olivia, you are truly my rainbow baby, inspiring joy wherever you go. I delight in you.

Michael, thank you for building a family with me and for trusting me when I bring up yet another against-the-grain idea to try out. Your confidence and support—from the delivery room (or birthing tub) to nightly around the dinner table—have inspired boldness and strength. You make us better.

What a blast to raise babies with my brave, beautiful Mama Tribe! Katey Hellman, your early feedback on the manuscript solidified my resolve to see this book through. From swapping voice memos about our kids to sharing parenting book recs, you've inspired the inception of The School Zone Mentality before it had a name. (And not just because we bonded over a shared outrage of strangers feeding our children candy.) Alexandria Gorda, you are my biggest cheerleader and fiercest friend. Fortitude, sister.

Meagan Zachary, we literally raised our babies together, and your intuitive approach to motherhood is beautiful to behold. Brennan Tucker, your practical advice and inspiring words helped me get the dang thing done.

Mom, you're so very loved and missed. I know you'd indulge your grandkids milkshakes for breakfast if you had the chance. Beth, thank you for filling some really big shoes and ensuring I never had to endure the newborn days without a mom to answer my late-night texts. Steve/Dad, thank you for giving everything you had to pave a runway for Bobby and me to succeed. To our Gonzalez-Rabon-Torres fam, raising our children surrounded by cousins, aunts/uncles, and grandparents on a regular basis is an actual dream. To our Pierce-Cottrell-Hilbert-Valladarez fam, thank you for seeing us through the loss of Biggie, and for carrying us to the other side where joy and new beginnings welcomed us.

Calling this book "self-published" feels like an incredible misnomer given the contributions of Teresa Lynn at Tranquility Press. Teresa, you were my publishing sherpa and rescued me from my own bossy tone. Your edits no doubt saved many exhausted fellow parents from chucking this book, and your formatting brought my vision to life. Thank you again to my husband for letting me rope you into producing the audiobook via Peak Sound Productions. (Not sorry for hitting on the sound guy.) And huge thanks to Randy Peterson at The Distillery Media for capturing a headshot that truly felt like me. (The fake laugh plays, every time.)

I must recognize the talented professionals and authors who leveled-up my own parenting and informed the ideas in this book, either explicitly or implicitly: Kim John Payne and Lisa Ross, Drs. Daniel Siegel and Tina Payne Bryson, Dr. Gordon Neufeld, Dr. Gabor Maté, Dr. Leonard Sax, Dr. William Stixrud and Ned Johnson, Dr. Elisa Song, Justin Whitmel Earley, Dr. Anna Lembke,

Dr. Jonathan Haidt, Dr. Deborah MacNamara, Tony Wagner, Ted Dintersmith, Sissy Goff, Dr. Kathy Koch, Julie Bogart, Ben Sasse, James Clear, and John Holt.

Jesus, thank you for rescuing this sinner and giving her the most beautiful life. It's all yours.

ABOUT THE AUTHOR

Natalie Gonzalez grew up in sunny Carlsbad, CA. Pale-legged and frizzy-haired, she could always be found with her nose in a book or a pen in her hand. She studied writing and cultural studies at Pratt Institute and obtained a Sociology degree from Texas Christian University. She currently resides in Burleson, Texas with her husband Michael, son Asher, and daughter Olivia, living the simple suburban dream (minivan included).

The School Zone Mentality is Natalie's first book.

www.ingramcontent.com/pod-product-compliance
Lightning Source LLC
Chambersburg PA
CBHW021111130626
46554CB00002B/631